A LABOR OF LOVE

A LABOR OF LOVE
THE 1946 EUROPEAN MISSION OF
EZRA TAFT BENSON

Deseret Book Company
Salt Lake City, Utah

Library of Congress Catalog Card No. 89-85935

ISBN 0-87579-275-8

Printed in the United States of America

10   9   8   7   6   5   4   3   2

CONTENTS

FOREWORD

This is a story about love—the love of a man for the Lord; the love between a man and a woman and the support they give each other; the compassion of human beings one for another; the caring of the Brethren for a colleague an ocean away performing a mission of mercy; and God's overarching love above all.

In December 1945, Elder Ezra Taft Benson was called to serve as president of the European Mission. But this was no ordinary mission call. World War II had left the Church's organizational structure crippled, and almost all contact between Church headquarters and the European Saints had been severed during the long years of war. Many Saints had been driven from their homes, lost loved ones, and owned nothing more than what they wore on their backs. Some were in advanced stages of starvation.

Elder Benson's assignment was to travel throughout Europe, locate the Saints, direct the distribution of welfare supplies where needed, arrange for missionary work to commence again on the continent, and essentially try to repair the extensive spiritual, temporal, and emotional damage the war had caused the Saints there. This book tells the story of how it all unfolded.

Why focus a book on just one year?

Because the year selected is of such an unusual nature,

and was so demanding for both President Benson and his wife, who was called on to support her husband and keep things running smoothly at home with their six children while he was in Europe, that their priorities and depth of testimonies come into clear focus. And because the essence of the gospel of Jesus Christ is poignantly displayed in one circumstance after another.

This book is an account of President Benson's mission of mercy to the European Saints. It tells the story of what he found there, of those he blessed and comforted, of Saints throughout the world who joined together to help each other in tragic circumstances, of those who offered invaluable support at home and abroad, and of a kind Providence who oversaw it all and poured out miracles.

After nearly eleven months in Europe, Elder Benson returned home. He summarized the remarkable experience he'd had: "Our great desire was to live so that the Lord would bless us in carrying out those directions, and I testify that the Lord has in very deed blessed us on every turn. He has gone before us. Barriers have melted away. Problems that seemed impossible to solve have been solved, and the work in large measure has been accomplished through the blessings of the Lord."

This book demonstrates that a testimony of Jesus Christ will prevail over something as terrible as war and bring the Saints through triumphant. It shows what happens when loving individuals in trying circumstances devote themselves to the Lord and to each other.

EXPLANATION OF SOURCES

The materials quoted in this book include the personal journals of Ezra Taft Benson (cited in the text as ETB Journal) and Flora Amussen Benson (FAB Journal), correspondence between the two (ETB to FAB, and vice versa), the European Mission History, the *Church News* and the *Improvement Era,* and some personal recollections of Ezra Taft Benson, referred to as ETB Reminiscences.

The editorial mechanics in the preparation of this material have been minimal. A few omissions of personal material have been made. Also, repetitive material has been edited for readability. Some spelling and grammatical errors have been silently corrected. This is intended as a personal rather than a historical record.

PROLOGUE:
END OF WAR AND
PREPARATION FOR MISSION

Tuesday, May 8, 1945: President Harry S Truman announced this morning at seven the official unconditional surrender of all German forces. (ETB Journal.)

President Heber J. Grant had the floodlights of the exterior of the Salt Lake Temple, darkened during the war, turned on. (*Improvement Era,* January 1946, page 10.)

Shortly after the close of World War II, President George Albert Smith was the President of the Church. The reports from Europe indicated great suffering among our people and the people generally. There was a shortage of food, clothing, fuel, transportation—a shortage of almost everything required for civilized living. (ETB Reminiscences.)

THURSDAY, SEPTEMBER 20, 1945:
SALT LAKE CITY, UTAH

Elder John A. Widtsoe reported that he had received a letter from the president of the northernmost branch of the Church in Narvik, Norway, who reported the destruction of his home and the death of his wife as a result of the bombing.

Near the close of his letter, this man said that if any

1

of the Brethren had a pair of shoes or two of his size, he could use them very well. He said further that his children had no clothing. (ETB Reminiscences.)

THURSDAY, OCTOBER 18, 1945:
SALT LAKE CITY, UTAH

Most important of the steps being taken to lend spiritual and temporal succor to the Saints in the war-ravished countries was the appointment of two of the General Authorities to go immediately to Europe. Elder John A. Widtsoe of the Council of the Twelve and Elder Thomas E. McKay, Assistant to the Council of the Twelve, both of whom have had wide experience in Europe, received this assignment from the First Presidency.

They expect to make contact with all European missions and to direct aid to individual Saints who are reported to be suffering from lack of food and clothing. Elders Widtsoe and McKay expect to be gone for several months, possibly a full year, on this assignment. They are to go alone as soon as the transportation can be arranged.

Other action to assure relief from suffering of members of the Church in Europe was taken this week by a committee of Church leaders assigned the task of finding ways and means to send food and clothing to those in need.

Already this week hundreds of packages containing needed food and clothing are being sent by mail to Europe. The full facilities of the Church welfare program, including its stocks of food, clothing, and bedding, are at the disposal of this committee to give aid to European Saints. The committee is also exhausting all possibilities of finding shipping space for large quantities of such items for the Saints of Europe. At present the packages, limited in weight by postal regulations, are being directed to branch presidents and some individuals in several European countries.

When larger stores are sent to Europe by the Church, it will be one of the tasks of Elders Widtsoe and McKay to direct distribution and facilitate the movement of the cloth-

2

PROLOGUE:
END OF WAR AND
PREPARATION FOR MISSION

Tuesday, May 8, 1945: President Harry S Truman announced this morning at seven the official unconditional surrender of all German forces. (ETB Journal.)

President Heber J. Grant had the floodlights of the exterior of the Salt Lake Temple, darkened during the war, turned on. (*Improvement Era,* January 1946, page 10.)

Shortly after the close of World War II, President George Albert Smith was the President of the Church. The reports from Europe indicated great suffering among our people and the people generally. There was a shortage of food, clothing, fuel, transportation—a shortage of almost everything required for civilized living. (ETB Reminiscences.)

THURSDAY, SEPTEMBER 20, 1945:
SALT LAKE CITY, UTAH

Elder John A. Widtsoe reported that he had received a letter from the president of the northernmost branch of the Church in Narvik, Norway, who reported the destruction of his home and the death of his wife as a result of the bombing.

Near the close of his letter, this man said that if any

1

of the Brethren had a pair of shoes or two of his size, he could use them very well. He said further that his children had no clothing. (ETB Reminiscences.)

THURSDAY, OCTOBER 18, 1945:
SALT LAKE CITY, UTAH

Most important of the steps being taken to lend spiritual and temporal succor to the Saints in the war-ravished countries was the appointment of two of the General Authorities to go immediately to Europe. Elder John A. Widtsoe of the Council of the Twelve and Elder Thomas E. McKay, Assistant to the Council of the Twelve, both of whom have had wide experience in Europe, received this assignment from the First Presidency.

They expect to make contact with all European missions and to direct aid to individual Saints who are reported to be suffering from lack of food and clothing. Elders Widtsoe and McKay expect to be gone for several months, possibly a full year, on this assignment. They are to go alone as soon as the transportation can be arranged.

Other action to assure relief from suffering of members of the Church in Europe was taken this week by a committee of Church leaders assigned the task of finding ways and means to send food and clothing to those in need.

Already this week hundreds of packages containing needed food and clothing are being sent by mail to Europe. The full facilities of the Church welfare program, including its stocks of food, clothing, and bedding, are at the disposal of this committee to give aid to European Saints. The committee is also exhausting all possibilities of finding shipping space for large quantities of such items for the Saints of Europe. At present the packages, limited in weight by postal regulations, are being directed to branch presidents and some individuals in several European countries.

When larger stores are sent to Europe by the Church, it will be one of the tasks of Elders Widtsoe and McKay to direct distribution and facilitate the movement of the clothin which Saints in Germany, particularly, are found, which lend urgency to the need for a smooth and complete functioning of the Church welfare program. (*Church News.*)

TUESDAY, OCTOBER 30-TUESDAY, NOVEMBER 13, 1945: WASHINGTON, D.C.

President George Albert Smith and a delegation of the Brethren traveled to Washington, D.C., to inquire firsthand about conditions in the various countries of Europe and how best to proceed in arranging for distribution of Church relief supplies.

They visited with Cabinet members and other national and international dignitaries, including Harry S Truman, President of the United States. President Truman was congenial and helpful; however, he was surprised at the response of the President of the Church when asked how much time would be required for the Church to collect items for distribution.

President Smith quickly replied, "We have already collected clothing and food and are ready at once to begin shipping supplies." He then explained the details of the Church welfare program. (ETB Reminiscences.)

SATURDAY, DECEMBER 1, 1945: SALT LAKE CITY, UTAH

Perhaps the most critical need facing Europe is fuel. It is necessary that the little available be used for the running of the trains and the factories. Homes and dwelling places are not heated or heated poorly, and the slightest use of hot water is a luxury. There is little fuel even for cooking. In many of the overrun countries the stoves, pots, and pans, were taken by the Nazis for the making of munitions. Unless the people are immediately clothed against the cold winter, suffering will be intense.

Realizing that this is a real opportunity to help our brothers and sisters, the directing heads of the program are anxious that the best of clothing and shoes be donated.

5

How bitter their disappointment will be, and how imprudent to waste time and money, if articles are sent that are not serviceable.

While the dire need for clothing and bedding is being met, food is also being shipped in increasing amounts during the winter. The harvest in Europe has been poor and small this fall. The diets of all have been meager and insufficient for adequate nutrition. The greatest need is for fats. Most of the fats available during the past war years have been used in the making of ammunition. The welfare program will endeavor to supply this lack through the various meat-producing projects. The second need is for vitamins. For some years at least two stakes have produced vitamins as their part of the budget assignment. In addition to their production, it will be necessary to make commercial purchases to supply the demand.

Little did the Prophet Joseph Smith realize when the Lord revealed to him the storehouse program for taking care of those in need that a hundred and fourteen years later it would mean the temporal salvation for his people in Europe. And little, too, did the members of the Church realize when the First Presidency announced in 1936 the organization of the welfare program to assist the bishops and the branch presidents in the discharge of their duties "in searching after the poor to administer to their wants" that their work on welfare projects, in the production and storage of the necessities of life, would, in less than a decade, help to bring relief to a war-torn world. (*Improvement Era,* December 1945, page 747.)

SATURDAY, DECEMBER 22, 1945:
SALT LAKE CITY, UTAH

President Smith called a special meeting of the First Presidency and the Council of the Twelve in their office. The Twelve were seated around the table with the First Presidency at the head at a cross table.

After the prayer President Smith referred to the fact

that announcement had been made that Brothers Widtsoe and McKay would go to Europe, but he said that on further investigation they found conditions so bad in Europe that it would not be wise to send these two brethren, but to select a younger man.

Elder Harold B. Lee tells the story: "I began quickly to look around the table, speculating as to who would be called. One of the first men I eliminated was Elder Benson, who had the largest family as well as the youngest. I'd not quite made my survey around the table when President Smith announced that they had decided to call Elder Benson to go to Europe." (ETB Reminiscences.)

After outlining the magnitude of the job, President Smith announced that I had been chosen to go and preside over the European Mission and take charge also of the distribution of relief help for our people in those war-torn countries.

It came as a great shock, and I was asked what my wife would say to my leaving her with a young family. I assured the Brethren that I could always count on my wife's full support in any call from the Church.

The meeting then ratified unanimously President Smith's nomination. Now I am to put my affairs in order promptly and go to Washington, D.C., to try and get the necessary permit and transportation to England. (ETB Journal.)

President Smith said: "I am not at all concerned about you. You will be just as safe there as anywhere else in the world if you take care of yourself, and you will be able to accomplish a great work." (ETB Reminiscences.)

Later in a sweet and impressive talk with my wife, sanctified by tears, Flora expressed loving gratitude and assured me of her wholehearted support. At dinner I told

7

the children, who were surprised, interested, and fully loyal. (ETB Journal.)

SATURDAY, DECEMBER 29, 1945:
SALT LAKE CITY, UTAH

First notices that the welfare packages being sent to Europe by the Church for the relief of destitute members of the Church are being received in good condition—and are bringing happiness to many people—have been received this week at the Church Offices.

The first words of thanks received have come from Holland. This country was the first to which the packages of bedding, clothing, and foodstuffs were sent. All of the letters express thanks for the needed items, but also contain expressions of faith and thankfulness for the peace that has come.

Some interesting excerpts from the letters are printed herewith: "Utrecht, Holland—Thank you very much for all you have sent to help us. We have received your parcel (and also other members in our town) in good condition, and we are very thankful for all that you have sent—especially for the shoes, the soap, and the clothes for the children. We had shoes no more, but now we can go to our work and to church. Now we need not wash us with sand-soap, but with good American soap. We are also thankful to our Lord for what He has given us by your welfare committee. This year we have the best Christmas of the last six years."

It is estimated that a total of over 7,000 of these packages of clothing, bedding, and much needed articles have been sent from the Church welfare centers in America to the Latter-day Saint families in Europe. (*Church News.*)

SUNDAY, DECEMBER 30, 1945:
SALT LAKE CITY, UTAH

I was told by the President that I could select my own secretary to go with me. I went through the list of returned missionaries of the past five years from Germany because I wanted someone who could speak German. Based on the records, I selected Frederick W. Babbel.

I did not know Brother Babbel—I'd never heard of him, but on inquiry found that he was in the military at the Presidio in San Francisco, California.

I got him on the telephone and asked him how he would like to go with me as my secretary and companion to Europe, without our wives, on an emergency mission of indefinite duration.

He immediately said, "I would be glad to go with you anywhere, Brother Benson!"

In two weeks we had him cleared for service in the Church. (ETB Reminiscences.)

MONDAY, DECEMBER 31, 1945:
SALT LAKE CITY, UTAH

The next year will no doubt be spent in large measure, and possibly in its entirety, abroad. It will mean some sacrifice of material comforts. I will miss my wife and sweet children and the association of the Brethren and the visits to the stakes.

I go, however, with no fear whatsoever, knowing that this is the Lord's work and that He will sustain me. I am grateful for the opportunity, and deeply grateful my wife, who is always most loyal, feels the same way. God bless them while I am away. (ETB Journal.)

THURSDAY, JANUARY 3-TUESDAY, JANUARY 8, 1946:
WASHINGTON, D.C.

Spent time in Washington, D.C., working on passports, transportation, etc., pertaining to my trip to Europe. (ETB Journal.)

FRIDAY, JANUARY 4, 1946:
WASHINGTON, D.C.

The Lord has surely opened the way today. I've not only seen the officials at the Department of State, but got my passport, which usually takes thirty days, and visas for Great Britain, France, and Holland, which usually takes days. (ETB to FAB.)

TUESDAY, JANUARY 22, 1946:
SALT LAKE CITY, UTAH

Office. Evening attended a party of the General Authorities in the Lion House, where Elders Kimball, Petersen, Cowley, and myself rendered three quartet numbers. It was a lovely party, and kind reference was made in word, song, and prayer to my forthcoming trip. (ETB Journal.)

SUNDAY, JANUARY 27, 1946:
SALT LAKE CITY, UTAH

I shall never forget this Sabbath day. After the morning at the office and a dinner at home with just the family, we all gathered in the study for a little sacred period together.

After singing "We Thank Thee, O God, for a Prophet," Reed, my oldest son, led in prayer. I then gave a few words of counsel and commendation, and then I gave each child a blessing as the Spirit directed.

I invited Reed and Mark to lay on hands with me as we blessed little Beth, seventeen months. Then we put her in for her nap, after which I blessed each child starting with the oldest, and then blessed my devoted wife, Flora.

We shed many tears of gratitude, even to the youngest one present—Bonnie, age five. We all felt strongly the sweet influence of the Spirit of the Lord with us. (ETB Journal.)

MONDAY, JANUARY 28, 1946:
SALT LAKE CITY, UTAH

Office all day. Last-minute preparations for European trip. Some good-byes were said and much love expressed.

Had a sweet visit with President George F. Richards, and as we parted we kissed each other a fond good-bye. He is a great soul. God bless him forever. How I pray I may see him on my return and live worthy of his association in the eternal worlds.

The First Presidency, with President Smith as voice, set me apart. Flora was present. [See Appendix for text of blessing.] (ETB Journal.)

After the setting apart, the Presidency greeted us warmly, and President Clark spoke encouragingly and in praise of Flora. Among other things, he said, in response to her statement regarding devoted women of the past, "There is none better than you."

How true he spoke, for truly in all my acquaintances I have never met a more completely devoted woman with greater faith in the purposes of the Almighty or with a stronger testimony of the truth or a greater desire to do everything in her power to build up the kingdom of God on the earth. (ETB Journal.)

Spent a pleasant evening with the five junior members of the Twelve and their wives in the home of President J. Reuben Clark. Flora and I were shown much love and affection, and our hearts had much to be grateful for. (ETB Journal.)

PART 1:
DEPARTURE AND MISSION

TUESDAY, JANUARY 29, 1946:
SALT LAKE CITY, UTAH

Today will always be remembered with deep gratitude.
I spent most of the day at the office. Many called to wish
me Godspeed on my mission. Everyone is so kind — neighbors, friends, the Brethren, etc. Many have brought gifts.

I was in conferences with members of the First Presidency several times. How I love them and appreciate their
love and confidence. May I ever be worthy of it.

Several of the Brethren have wanted to drive me to the
airport, but I've accepted Brother Lee's invitation. I feel so
close to him — a boyhood schoolmate and beloved associate. I had dinner and sweet devotion with the family at
home and packed up my bags, received callers, completed
details, and entertained many soul-satisfying thoughts.

At 9:40 P.M. good-byes were said to my three daughters — Barbara, Beverly, Bonnie — and son Mark. We were
sobbing with sweet emotion. We also called Reed at Provo
and talked until we both choked up. I had previously
hugged little Beth good-bye as she put her sweet little arms
around my neck. (ETB Journal.)

When our daddy kissed and said good-bye to five of his children, they all cried and clung to him because of the great love they have for him. Our son, Reed, is attending school at BYU in Provo. His daddy called him long distance, and they were both so happy to talk to each other and say good-bye with much love and appreciation for each other. (FAB Journal.)

Leaving my children in tears pulled at my heartstrings, but there was not a murmur nor complaint. They are surely true blue.

May the Lord keep and bless my loved ones forever. I leave them in His kind and loving care with gratitude and confidence that He will ever be near them. (ETB Journal.)

Just before my husband's departure President George Albert Smith came to our home to say good-bye to my husband. He kissed him in fond embrace. (FAB Journal.)

Brother and Sister Harold B. Lee called for us at 10:00 P.M. and drove us to the airport where, to our surprise, we found Brothers and Sisters Spencer W. Kimball, Mark E. Petersen, Matthew Cowley, and others.

I bade my dear wife and friends a fond adieu. It was most difficult to tell my sweet and ever-loyal wife good-bye. (ETB Journal.)

It was a peaceful feeling which came over me when I fondly kissed and said good-bye to my devoted and loving husband. (FAB Journal.)

On the plane, as I reflected on the scenes of the last few days, I quietly shed tears of gratitude as we soared eastward on the plane. (ETB Journal.)

Our beloved father and husband left by plane to take up his duties as president of the European Mission. This is an exceed-

Members of the Council of the Twelve and their wives gathered at the airport to give Elder Benson a warm sendoff: (left to right) Frederick W. Babbel, Sister Babbel, Matthew Cowley, Flora A. Benson, Ezra Taft Benson, Emma Marr Petersen, Harold B. Lee, Camilla Kimball, Elva Cowley, Mark E. Petersen, Fern Lee, and Spencer W. Kimball.

ingly great call, and we as a family feel that our devoted father and husband was rightly chosen by the Lord to be called to this great and important work.

He shall be able to do a great and mighty work with the Lord as his constant companion. I don't know of a man that lives closer to the Lord than does my good husband. (FAB Journal.)

WEDNESDAY, JANUARY 30, 1946: NORTH PLATTE, NEBRASKA

At 6:00 A.M. we were grounded in North Platte due to bad weather. After careful checking and prayerful consideration, we decided to seek train space to Chicago. (ETB Journal.)

THURSDAY, JANUARY 31, 1946: CHICAGO, ILLINOIS, AND NEW YORK CITY

At Chicago the next morning, the president of the Chicago Stake met us with flight tickets on the plane to New York.

President Benson
and his secretary,
Fred Babbel, left Salt
Lake City during a
snowstorm.

Upon arriving in New York, we learned that the flight from New York to London was being postponed from Friday until the following day. (ETB Journal.)

FRIDAY, FEBRUARY 1, 1946:
NEW YORK CITY

Our flight was postponed twice today because of bad weather. It now appears we'll not leave until Sunday morning.

Spent the day making preparations and contacting foreign consuls and departments of government. (ETB Journal.)

Arrangements have now been consummated whereby

15

relief supplies may be sent in carload lots instead of individual gift packages as has been the practice. Several active relief agencies of other denominations and societies have pledged their full cooperation with the Church program and have expressed their admiration for the farsighted program that has been launched by the Church. (ETB to FAB.)

Today I had my first experience with a puncture on the car. I am beginning to realize that our daddy's absence is being greatly missed in so many ways, but we know it is the will of the Lord for him to go to the far countries of Europe to help those poor, suffering, worthy Saints, after such a terrible war, and to preach the glorious gospel to those who have not heard its truths. (FAB Journal.)

SUNDAY, FEBRUARY 3, 1946:
NEW YORK CITY AND GANDER, NEWFOUNDLAND

We arrived at the airport, checked with baggage and express agencies and customs, and left in a four-motored Clipper.

Weather was quite calm, after two days of storm, as we skirted the coast of Maine and Massachusetts and on up the coast to Gander, Newfoundland.

Two motors had been running "rough," so we stopped for checking and replacing spark plugs before starting across the Atlantic.

The ride was rough in spots, and some little anxiety was felt as we watched the engineer flash lights onto the two rough motors throughout the night as though all was not right.

We traveled blind part of the way. Sometimes it would clear until we could see the stars above and the water waves below, and then we'd go into clouds and have it a bit rough for a spell. (ETB Journal.)

Monday, February 4, 1946:
Ireland and London, England

We landed in Ireland on the banks of the River Shannon. After a breakfast of porridge, bacon, and eggs, we looked over the countryside while the mechanics took water from the magneto and then left for London.

Upon arrival in England, we checked regarding passports and with customs, had lunch (rather skimpy), and drove to the railway station, where we left by train for London. (ETB Journal.)

Along the way we observed many areas and buildings devastated by bombings, but the trip to the British Mission headquarters, which took us through one of the more severely bombed districts of London, forcibly arrested our attention to the destructiveness and futility of war.

It was indeed a happy moment to be greeted by President and Sister Hugh B. Brown and family, now supervising the activities of the British Mission, and to find them well and cheerful in spite of all of them having suffered somewhat as a result of the influenza epidemic that is becoming quite widespread.

In receiving a report of the British Mission, it was learned that most of the British Saints have weathered the terrific strain of war years and are still loyal and devoted to the Church.

People generally are quite downcast and apprehensive of the future. Many express fears of an even more terrible conflagration in the near future, but the Saints as a whole are quite optimistic and cheerful.

Although members are still in a scattered condition, the casualties of war among our members have been quite nominal. All are eagerly looking forward to the day when missionaries will again return to their midst.

Food and clothing are being severely rationed, and living conditions are much more critical than during the last year of the war. The many packages received by the Saints through the Church welfare program have filled a very great need and have given the Saints new hope and courage.

Much distress has been alleviated through the Church welfare program, and the packages which the Saints have received and are daily receiving have manifested in very deed the brotherly love and affection that binds the Church together. Grateful appreciation from Saints in all parts of the mission is being expressed daily.

It is difficult to understand the vast difference in conditions in America and in England without seeing and experiencing it. Food, clothing, and housing are desperately critical. Many people have become quite pessimistic and somewhat discouraged. Helpless indifference has replaced the usually cheerful disposition of some, but the Saints as a whole are quite outstanding for their resolute courage and faith in the future. (European Mission History.)

The contrast of conditions here with conditions in the States makes one feel that he is truly in another world. Everything seems short — including patience. England has truly felt the effects of this terrible war. (European Mission History.)

I received my first letter from my precious husband. It was a grand, spiritual, uplifting letter. I am so thankful to be blessed with such a righteous man whose life has been and is a perfect example of all that is virtuous, clean, honest, fine and manly — wanting always for his wife and children to be cared for in the best manner, wanting them to have the best he can provide. The most treasured possession which he leaves his family is a wonderful heritage. Above all, he wants his family to have a strong testimony of the gospel. He would and his wife would rather be penniless and be poor in this world's goods than to lose our faith and testimony in the gospel. (FAB Journal.)

TUESDAY, FEBRUARY 5, 1946:
LONDON, ENGLAND

First day in London. After a breakfast of thinned fruit juice and porridge, we left for the city. We first registered with the police, then called at the American Embassy.

We next visited the Commanding General of the United Kingdom Base Section regarding army vehicles and learned they are all "frozen." Visit was pleasant and profitable.

Spent evening dictating and writing letters. Received today the most soul-satisfying and inspiring letter from Flora. She is a great soul and as nearly perfect as I can imagine a companion to be. (ETB Journal.)

Brother Anderson from the Church offices (private secretary to President George Albert Smith) called and told me that the General Authorities had just received a telegram that our dear husband and daddy and his secretary arrived safely in London, England. Brother Anderson said it was impossible for them to telephone or cable to us in Salt Lake because of strikes. (FAB Journal.)

WEDNESDAY, FEBRUARY 6, 1946:
LONDON, ENGLAND

In view of the limitations on fuel, lights, food, all types of supplies, and in fact most everything, together with the fact that President Brown and family are already crowded, it seemed best not to try and squeeze in with them if we can get other quarters. Then, too, I believe we will operate most efficiently during the ensuing few months especially if we can be in the business section close to transportation concerns and government agencies with whom we will need to deal rather frequently. (European Mission History.)

Left early for the city, where we visited several prospective office and living quarters. The rents are exorbitantly high, and yet we must be in a respectable neighborhood near the agencies with which we will have to deal if we are to be most efficient.

We finally settled on a ground floor flat in the Mayfair section, only a block from Grosvenor Square where the American Embassy and other U.S. offices are located.

Visited officials at the embassy and made arrangements to use U.S. American Transport Command (ATC) planes for transportation to Continental countries, where they operate, and in other cases the British Overseas Airways Corporation (BOAC). (ETB Journal.)

THURSDAY, FEBRUARY 7, 1946:
LONDON, ENGLAND

Moved into our flat. (ETB Journal.)

We are quite comfortably located. Our flat consists of two bedrooms, a bath, and a sitting room. We plan to use the facilities as a combination living quarters and offices. I believe they will serve very adequately for the immediate months ahead.

Although in our search for a place we received nothing but discouragement — and on our first day our efforts were entirely futile — yet the Lord blessed us, and on the second day we had a choice of four different flats which were available to us. Prices are exorbitant. To the average Britisher the word *American* is synonymous with wealth. We are, however, learning a few safeguards and ways to economize. (ETB to FAB.)

In the evening accepted invitation of President and Sister Brown and enjoyed a Tchaikovsky concert by the London Philharmonic Orchestra in the Royal Albert Hall. The place was practically filled. There are seven floor levels. It was a brilliant and inspiring performance. Thank the Lord for great music!

While at the musical, received one of Flora's encouraging and soul-satisfying letters. (ETB Journal.)

Today I missed three parties I was invited to. The children's health and keeping the home in order are far more important than parties.

President J. Reuben Clark talked to me over the phone and said to let him know if he could do anything for me at any time. He said I was the most independent woman he ever knew. He said, "It's the hardest thing to get the chance to do anything for you!" (FAB Journal.)

FRIDAY, FEBRUARY 8, 1946:
LONDON, ENGLAND

Conferences today with agricultural attache for the United Kingdom; also with European news manager of United Press. Conferred with several officials at American Embassy regarding transportation to continental Europe. Later I talked to Paris regarding purchase of autos for mission presidents and purchase of a French Mission headquarters, etc. Made plans for trip to the Continent next week. (ETB Journal.)

SATURDAY, FEBRUARY 9, 1946:
LONDON, ENGLAND

In cooperation with the priorities division of the American Embassy, I received priorities for airplane travel to Paris and return. Also obtained necessary British visas and tickets on ATC planes.

I obtained my food ration book. We had dinner in our rooms from food allowed from our rations consisting of bread, butter, cheese, jam, milk, and one-third of a candy bar. We enjoyed it much. (ETB Journal.)

SUNDAY, FEBRUARY 10, 1946:
LONDON, ENGLAND

In office in study. Talked on telephone with acting president of Danish Mission, Orson B. West. This was his first contact with anyone from Zion. His first words were, "God bless you. Welcome to Europe!" (ETB Journal.)

MONDAY, FEBRUARY 11, 1946:
LONDON, ENGLAND, AND PARIS, FRANCE

Reported at office of European Air Transport Service (EATS) and was driven to the airport. After clearing customs, passport section, etc., I boarded a C-54 ATC plane with eleven other passengers, all male, and left London for Paris. The plane was an army transport with a metal bench along each side and no conveniences except parachutes.

In one hour and forty-five minutes we arrived in Paris via Dieppe. (ETB Journal.)

The day was spent in trying to purchase surplus army cars for use of mission presidents, inspecting property for a possible mission home for the French Mission, and visiting Saints. (ETB Journal.)

The history and progress of the French Mission during the war years was given by Brother Jean Kleinert, who carried on in charge of the Church activities in Paris. It was learned that the Saints as a whole are quite well and anxiously looking forward to the return of missionaries to labor among them.

Many Church welfare packages have been received by the members and have filled a very great need for food and clothing, which is still very critical. Most of the members are now quite well provided with bedding and clothing, but the need for additional food is still quite apparent.

Missionary work has been carried on quite effectively during the course of the war, chiefly through the efforts of the splendid servicemen's group in Paris. Most of the servicemen have now left the Paris area. Those who remain, however, are continuing to do a splendid missionary work. (European Mission History.)

President Benson met with LDS servicemen wherever he traveled, including Chaplain Howard C. Badger and Captain Thomas Adams in Paris.

Today I received a lovely box of chocolates sent by my husband from New York just before he flew for London, England. The card said, "To the loveliest most loyal companion in all the world. Am thinking of you my last night in the good old USA. Lovingly. 'T' " (FAB Journal.)

TUESDAY, FEBRUARY 12, 1946:
PARIS, FRANCE

Completed arrangements for the purchase of seven one-half-ton Dodge pick-up trucks and arranged to drive one to Holland tomorrow. (ETB Journal.)

Sister Spencer W. Kimball called to ask me to go to the show with her tonight. It was kind of her, but I felt I should stay home. Sister Mark E. Petersen called and asked if I would go to a

basketball game with her. I thanked her also for her thoughtfulness.
(FAB Journal.)

WEDNESDAY, FEBRUARY 13, 1946:
PARIS, FRANCE

Arose early and worked in room for an hour. We
checked on several matters incident to our trip to The
Hague in Holland. Spent most of morning arranging with
the military authorities for gas to drive the one car to Holland.

We planned to start on our journey, but a careful checking showed the front bearings of the car badly worn and
unfit to drive. We made arrangements for train travel in
the morning. (ETB Journal.)

THURSDAY, FEBRUARY 14, 1946:
PARIS, FRANCE, AND THE HAGUE, NETHERLANDS

Left Paris and arrived in Brussels, Belgium, on a good
train. Left Brussels on a modern Belgian train and arrived
at Antwerp, where we changed to a local, old-fashioned
German short-car train. (ETB Journal.)

Rail conditions are still very bad on the Continent. It
was necessary to change trains several times and to take
an army truck on one stretch where bridges had been
blown up and on which repair had not yet been completed.

The train from Antwerp to The Hague was a small,
rickety, flat-wheeled model that showed signs of having
been reclaimed from the scrap heap. Fortunately it held
together and brought us safely to our destination. (European Mission History.)

The visits today with men on the train and in buses
revealed the terrible conditions through which Holland has
passed during the past five years. Young men spoke freely
of the underground army of which they were members

24

and of the hard but willing toil of their wives, mothers, and sisters.

I am greatly impressed with the quality of character of the Netherlands people. They have suffered much but seem cheerful and determined to come back. Many of them speak English from contact with the Yanks, but more from study as the children who go on with their education beyond thirteen are required to learn English, French, and German.

Much damage has been wrought in Rotterdam and The Hague particularly, and in fields near the cities one can see shell craters. Some have been filled in already; others were being filled as we passed, but even where crops have been planted the outline is still to be seen. (ETB Journal.)

FRIDAY, FEBRUARY 15, 1946:
THE HAGUE, NETHERLANDS, AND COPENHAGEN, DENMARK

After early breakfast at the Officers' Club, went to American Embassy. The transportation priorities man went with me to the KLM office, where we secured tickets.

Later I met with the mission presidency of Holland for over an hour. (ETB Journal.)

In checking on the history of the mission during the war, it was learned that the Saints have been very loyal and cooperated very closely with their leaders even under the most adverse conditions. The chapel in Rotterdam was destroyed, but the former mission headquarters at The Hague can be quickly repaired as soon as glass is available.

Great ingenuity on the part of the local brethren appointed to take charge of the mission was necessary in order to protect most of the Church property and funds from being confiscated by the German government. Nearly everything retained had to be cleverly concealed, and President Schipaanboord related many instances where his own life and that of some of the members was placed in jeopardy through the actions they found necessary to take in order to protect the property.

Brother P. Vlan was a German prisoner of war for nearly two years, during which time he converted six of his fellow prisoners to the gospel—all of whom are taking an active part in the mission. (European Mission History.)

Much of the critical need for food, clothing, and bedding has been filled through the generous number of relief packages received by the Saints from the Church welfare project. Food is still severely rationed, and many items of clothing are still quite difficult to obtain. (European Mission History.)

The consular's driver drove us to the airport in Amsterdam, where we took a plane for Copenhagen.

We went to the mission home, where we were received warmly. (ETB Journal.)

SATURDAY, FEBRUARY 16, 1946:
COPENHAGEN, DENMARK

This has been an interesting and profitable day. This morning we visited the famous Cathedral of Copenhagen (State Lutheran Church) or My Lady's Church, as it is also called. Here we saw the famous marble works by Thorvaldsen, Denmark's greatest sculptor, of Christ and the Twelve Apostles done in Rome 1820-40. We also saw in the two vestries "The Baptism of Christ" and "The Institution of the Last Supper."

I was interviewed by a man from the state-owned radio station who recorded our conversation which was broadcast to Denmark, Sweden, and Norway. (ETB Journal.)

Conditions generally in this mission are favorable. The most serious shortage is fuel. The welfare packages have been received and deeply appreciated. Food in Denmark is more plentiful now than probably any other war-torn country in Europe, and even during the war years our Saints did not go hungry. There seems now to be plenty of food, clothing, and bedding, except for linen, and of course this is scarce in most nations, including the United States.

None of the products received have entered the "black market," which is limited almost entirely to tobacco, liquors, and wines. During the war this mission fixed up many packages and sent them to the distressed Saints in Norway and Holland. This is but one indication of the close bond which exists between the Saints in the Scandinavian countries.

Membership has steadily increased, and the tithing of the Saints in the mission has more than doubled. (European Mission History.)

The Saints are in excellent physical and spiritual health. Everywhere we found an enthusiastic spirit of optimism. They are hopeful and are living the gospel more fully than ever before. During the occupation, only one of our members (inactive) was imprisoned; however, two of our Saints—a man and his wife without family—were shot as traitors by the underground movement in 1944 for, it is claimed, selling information to the enemy.

There are a few German refugee Saints still in Denmark. They are given sufficient freedom to permit them to attend our services regularly. (European Mission History.)

The outlook for missionary work in Denmark is good. During the war ten local missionaries were active throughout the mission, and their efforts were most successful. People are much more friendly toward the Church than ever before, and it appears that we are now becoming known for what we are and not for what our enemies have said about us. (European Mission History.)

At the bishops' storehouse on Welfare Square this week

four carloads of food and clothing were loaded outbound for New York where it will be shipped—two carloads to Norway and two to Holland to alleviate in a measure the suffering in those countries. Subsequent shipments are planned for the needy in other areas.

Two cars were loaded with canned fruit, vegetables, and milk, and the other two with articles of clothing of all kinds necessary to the comfort of the recipients.

The canned food was packed in strong wooden boxes secured by the General Welfare Commitee from the ordinance plant in Tooele. Originally used for the transportation of shell cases, they will now carry food to Europe, insuring its transportation and delivery in good shape. Such boxes may furnish a twofold purpose in that, having served the initial purpose, they may then be used for fuel in countries where that commodity is scarce indeed. (*Church News.*)

SUNDAY, FEBRUARY 17, 1946:
COPENHAGEN, DENMARK

I shall always have sweet memories of this day with the Saints in Copenhagen. Never have I witnessed greater devotion to the work and deeper love for the leaders of the Church.

At Sunday School the entire congregation stood as I entered. Then the president of the Copenhagen Branch welcomed me in fine English. The president of the mission Relief Society then presented me with a large bouquet of red tulips and white lilacs. I could not hold back the tears.

I spoke briefly to the children through an interpreter and took most of the class period to speak to the adults. There were 158 present. I blessed five sisters during the day.

At the evening service there were 515 present—at least 200 of whom were nonmembers. They were most attentive as I spoke for forty minutes on the Restoration. The music was beautiful. (ETB Journal.)

Before leaving this city, we visited the archives and the nearby city of Koge, the birthplace of Sister Benson's father. As a result of these visits, new genealogical information was uncovered and arrangements made with one of the local Church researchers to carry on with the work. Permission has now been secured to photograph on microfilm all of the genealogical records in this nation, and the Genealogical Society of the Church is now preparing to accomplish this work. (European Mission History.)

President George Albert Smith called by phone this evening to see how we were getting along. He said my husband had written him from London a fine letter. (FAB Journal.)

MONDAY, FEBRUARY 18, 1946:
COPENHAGEN, DENMARK, AND STOCKHOLM, SWEDEN

We drove about the city of Copenhagen, saw the famous Mermaid and the residential areas. After a good dinner at the mission home, we boarded the train for Stockholm, Sweden. It was hard to leave the dear Saints who have been so very kind to me the last three days. It seems I've known them for years. I shall never forget their kindness. (ETB Journal.)

TUESDAY, FEBRUARY 19, 1946:
STOCKHOLM, SWEDEN

We arrived in snow-covered Stockholm. During the day I held three press conferences with representatives of local leading papers. We were received kindly, and most favorable stories appeared in each case.

We held a public meeting with 200 people present, about 50 of whom were nonmembers. I spoke for thirty-five minutes through an interpreter and after the meeting stood at the door at the request of the people and shook hands with each. (ETB Journal.)

The fuel shortage in Sweden has been the biggest single

problem. It is still very acute. Many colds have resulted throughout the mission, but no serious epidemics have been encountered.

The day before our arrival was the first day people were allowed to heat water for bathing.

Food seems to be quite plentiful, and most of the Saints are now quite adequately supplied with most items of bedding and clothing. All express their appreciation for the assistance that has been rendered by the kindness of Saints at home.

It was learned that the Saints in Sweden had done much to help the Saints in Norway and Finland during the war by sending them items of food and clothing as often as was permissible.

The spiritual condition of our members is very fine. At the present time they have ten local members working as full-time missionaries, and the results have been most gratifying. Tithing has shown an increase of 300 percent during the war, of which amount a large portion has been paid by an increase of 50 percent in the number of Saints paying tithing. (European Mission History.)

WEDNESDAY, FEBRUARY 20, 1946:
STOCKHOLM, SWEDEN

This day we held a glorious meeting with the nine missionaries, branch presidents, and the mission president's family. I heard from each of those present.

The missionaries who have served full time for two years bore solemn testimony to the divinity of the work. All of us shed tears of gratitude as we were moved by the richness of the Spirit present.

We were especially touched by the opening remarks of President Fritz Johansson, who has served through the war years as acting mission president. He is small of stature but has a heart as big as the world. During last night and in the meeting, I felt impressed to call him to go on a mission to Finland as there were many people there who would accept the truth. (ETB Journal.)

The Church has one small branch in Finland. These Saints have been grievously impoverished by the war and are finding the welfare packages most helpful. C. Fritz Johansson was called to go as a missionary to Finland, to take a companion, and if possible to establish the work there so additional missionaries might be sent to this land to preach the gospel. It is hoped that this may lead to opening this land for increased missionary activities. (European Mission History.)

After taking some pictures and enjoying lunch, smorgasbord style, I spent two or three hours with the new and returning mission presidents and completed plans for the missionary work in Finland where we have a few members.

After dinner we walked to the railroad station with a large concourse of missionary Saints. They sang songs and bade us a fond farewell.

Never have I become more attached to any people in so short a time. May the Lord ever bless these faithful souls. (ETB Journal.)

THURSDAY, FEBRUARY 21, 1946:
STOCKHOLM, SWEDEN, AND OSLO, NORWAY

Arose early as the train stopped at the Norway-Sweden border. Was checked by customs of both countries. Water on the train was frozen solid.

Arrived in Oslo, Norway, and was greeted by Brother A. Richard Peterson, newly appointed mission president, and members of his family and those associated with him.

Attended a public meeting of the Oslo Branch and spoke through an interpreter for forty minutes. The choir and orchestra were unusually fine. There were 358 present—about 200 nonmembers. I shook hands with everyone at the door as they left. (ETB Journal.)

Here, as in other missions, very effective proselyting work has been carried on during the war and at the present time through local missionaries. More people have become converted to the gospel during the war years than in any other similar period of time, and the opportunities for a rich harvest are very bright. (European Mission History.)

The food situation in this and in other countries will no doubt improve greatly by next fall, providing of course that we have a favorable growing season this summer and fall. Until that time the food situation will likely become more acute all over Europe.

The Saints would welcome some packaged starches for cooking and laundry use and also some Cream of Wheat cereals for use of the children. Fats and jams have been particularly appreciated and could be profitably used in larger quantities.

An amusing thing happened when some of the Saints commented, on seeing the dried corn, that the General Authorities were most thoughtful in sending grain for the birds. They have, however, learned how to use corn in the diet. We learned also that one parcel had a package of cigarettes enclosed, which caused some amusement. (European Mission History.)

FRIDAY, FEBRUARY 22, 1946:
OSLO, NORWAY, AND COPENHAGEN, DENMARK

After breakfast we went to the Royal Air Force (RAF) office and then drove up on the mountain to the ski jump and got a good view of the city. Left Oslo for Copenhagen.

Our ride was the coldest I ever expect to make. There was no heat in the plane, and at 6,000 feet with ice, snow, and water below, it was a cold ride. Some of the men took their shoes off and rubbed their feet to keep the blood circulating. I kept my feet moving constantly for two hours and fared fairly well. (ETB Journal.)

In all of the missions visited to date, it is impossible to move funds out of the country either to America or to any European country. Some of the missions, particularly in the case of Norway, have had considerable difficulty holding onto our funds during the war period. In some cases the funds had to be shifted from bank to bank many times.

Mission literature generally is very much depleted. In all of the Scandinavian missions, I found the leadership and the members very anxious to have the Doctrine and Covenants in complete form translated into their respective languages, or at least into one of the three languages which might be used by all three of the missions.

During the war period, local missionaries — called for a period of two or more years — have performed an outstanding service. It has seemed to me during our visit in Europe thus far that, with the world in such an unsettled condition, we should ever keep in mind the training of local leadership in preparation for any future emergency which may again leave our missions without leadership from Zion.

The general condition of the Saints is much improved each day. Spiritually it has been good throughout the war and was perhaps never better than it is now. Mission leaders everywhere report that in their experience the Saints have never so completely lived the law of tithing and kept the Word of Wisdom and otherwise maintained the standards of the Church. While the Saints have been called upon to endure hardships almost beyond description in many cases, yet they have remained hopeful and optimistic, even during occupation of their countries by a foreign enemy when at times they feared for their very lives. (European Mission History.)

Traveling in unheated planes registering temperatures

as low as twenty degrees below zero and in unheated trains across the snow-covered landscape of the Scandinavian countries is all part of the day's work in our tour of the European missions. (European Mission History.)

But in every instance we were greeted upon arrival with such love and warmth of spirit that any hardships encountered in our travels were soon forgotten. Probably the gospel has never been so fully appreciated by the Saints in Europe as during the recent war period. Already we have come to love them deeply, and I am sure we cannot say enough in praise of their devotion to the truth and their love of the General Authorities of the Church. (European Mission History.)

Yale Ward reunion and dinner. It was very successful. I worked long and hard. (FAB Journal.)

SUNDAY, FEBRUARY 24, 1946:
COPENHAGEN, DENMARK

We have been held in Copenhagen all day due to the storm. At the airport all morning expecting to leave any time. The Danish airport officials made a desk available, so we got some work done. The afternoon was spent in study and rest at the mission home. In the evening I spoke to the Saints here for an hour through an interpreter. (ETB Journal.)

MONDAY, FEBRUARY 25, 1946:
COPENHAGEN, DENMARK, AND LONDON, ENGLAND

Left Copenhagen by plane and arrived in London. Stopped at British Mission office and picked up an armful of mail. Later spent the late afternoon and evening reading mail and dictating answers.

The sweet letters from my wife and children, all valentines from home, brought tears of joy and gratitude. (ETB Journal.)

Sent four packages to London to my husband. One was an eleven-pound box of soap, two boxes of candy, and one book. (FAB Journal.)

WEDNESDAY, FEBRUARY 27, 1946:
LONDON, ENGLAND

In London business district most of day working on passport, visas, transportation, customs, etc. Also made tentative arrangements to purchase an auto for use here and in the British Mission. Dictated and mailed twenty-five letters. (ETB Journal.)

THURSDAY, FEBRUARY 28, 1946:
LONDON, ENGLAND

London office dictating and working with customs, import licensing, and Fenton and Company regarding office supplies. Believe we have finally made our way through the tangle of red tape so our supplies, all of no commercial value and for relief and religious use, can be released. (European Mission History.)

The food situation in Europe is becoming more critical daily. The headlines this morning indicate that the rations in the British-occupied area have been ordered cut one-half — to 1,000 calories daily. Government officials here fear that riots and epidemics will follow.

My heart goes out to the Saints in the military areas. I am hopeful that before long the military authorities will amend their regulations to permit shipment of food and clothing into these areas. (ETB to FAB.)

FRIDAY, MARCH 1, 1946:
LONDON, ENGLAND

Transportation, welfare, and customs matters occupied most of the day. I talked with General McNarney's office in Frankfurt regarding possibility of getting relief into Germany to our Saints. Also conferred at length with two army

35

and navy officers who have just returned from Bremen and Berlin.

It is difficult to realize that agencies are forbidden to ship food into the occupied areas when people there are starving. (ETB Journal.)

It now appears that we will be able to place several cars of food and clothing in one of our own buildings where we have a family of our own people living who can assure the safety of the commodities stored. We have to be continually on the alert because of the extensive pilfering and stealing in all parts of Europe. (European Mission History.)

SUNDAY, MARCH 3, 1946:
LONDON, ENGLAND, AND DIEPPE, ROUEN, AND
PARIS, FRANCE

Left by boat-train for Paris after an unsuccessful attempt to take the plane earlier in the day. As we boarded the boat, we discovered that our first-class sleeping accommodations consisted of double-deck bunks placed end to end in groups of forty in what used to be lounging rooms.

The first-class passengers who followed us in the long line were either required to sleep in seats or required to stand all night after available seating space was used.

After all passengers were placed, we were able to secure very meager accommodations in a makeshift state room and crossed the Channel in comparative comfort. (ETB to FAB.)

Arrived at Dieppe, France. After a two-hour stop for customs, immigration, etc., we left for Paris.

As we went through Rouen, we saw on every side the ravages of war—bridges, highways, cathedrals, homes, etc., laid waste. We could see countless islands of black holes in the green pastures where bombs had missed their railway target.

36

Rebuilding has started, but years will be required to do the job. Dieppe Harbor was blown up by the retreating forces and is largely rubble. (ETB Journal.)

Dieppe, France, the scene of the European Theater's first commando raid, presented a desolate scene of bombing and destruction. Little reconstruction work has been undertaken thus far, and this scene was repeated in city after city as we rode on the train in Paris. The recent world conflict has left marks of devastation that may never be erased. Most of the passenger and railroad bridges have been destroyed, necessitating travel on hastily constructed wooden bridges. (European Mission History.)

We arrived at Paris and in an army truck were taken to the meeting of the Saints, where the meeting was already underway. I spoke to the thirty-five people assembled through an interpreter. (ETB Journal.)

Paris has recorded the heaviest snowfall since 1867, and many other areas in Europe find this sudden change in the weather very distressing because of the acute fuel shortage. (ETB to FAB.)

MONDAY, MARCH 4, 1946:
PARIS, FRANCE

Conferred today with government and transportation officials regarding purchase of two autos and transportation to other European countries. Also saw properties being proposed as French Mission home and office.

The city of Paris is a mass of slush following the fourteen-inch snow which set a record of many decades. (ETB Journal.)

Sister Matthias Cowley called. She is a grand spiritual lady. She is a temple worker. She reminds me so much of my dear sweet

37

Captain Brinton, President Benson, Captain Adams and Chaplain Badger pose in front of a newly purchased half-ton pickup truck.

mother. She is an inspiration, and we had a nice chat over the phone. (FAB Journal.)

FRIDAY, MARCH 8, 1946:
PARIS, FRANCE

Completed purchase of auto and took delivery of Citroen (four cylinders) at the Citroen Company. Drove car to various business conferences in Paris. (ETB Journal.)

SATURDAY, MARCH 9, 1946:
PARIS, FRANCE, AND BASEL, SWITZERLAND

Left Paris for Basel, Switzerland, by way of Verdun and Mannheim. At the latter place we stopped at the U.S. army base to have a tire fixed and eat lunch.

All along the way we saw heavy tanks and other equipment used in the Battle of the Bulge. Considerable bomb damage was in evidence in many of the cities, although the lovely fertile fields presented a most satisfying view.

The scene of devastation that greeted President Benson in Freiburg was to be repeated throughout Germany.

It was interesting to note the rural villages with home and barn in the same building and large well-built manure piles in each front yard. (ETB Journal.)

We arrived in Basel after passing French and Swiss customs and immigration officials and went to mission headquarters.

Switzerland, free from wars for 150 years, seems almost a different world. (ETB Journal.)

SUNDAY, MARCH 10, 1946:
BASEL, SWITZERLAND, AND KARLSRUHE, GERMANY

This day will stand out in my memory for years to come. It is my first day in the occupied areas of Germany.

After having some minor repairs made on the car, we left Basel for Karlsruhe via Freiburg and Offenburg. It was a pleasant ride through the picturesque and fertile fields, but my heart was made heavy as we drove through towns and cities leveled to the ground as a result of war. Occupation troops were everywhere. (ETB Journal.)

Along the way were scenes of horrible destruction. Many cities stand in almost complete ruin. The city of Freiburg presents a vast amount of devastation, and this scene was multiplied many times along the way.

People were going in groups to church, and we noticed especially that many of the children fled in terror at the approach of a car or at the sound of the horn. There was much evidence, however, that these people are clearing the ruins and rebuilding their cities and homes as rapidly as their meager supplies will permit. Not months, but years and decades will be required to do the job. (ETB to FAB.)

As we neared Karlsruhe, we entered the American Zone of occupation. Near the city were large pill boxes in small artificially made mounds which had been blown up by Allied bombs. It was heartrending to see beautiful Karlsruhe in ruins.

As we turned in the street where the meeting was to be held, it looked as if there was no building available to hold a meeting in—all seemed a pile of rubble. But by going back some distance, we finally located the place—a large building somewhat damaged from the bombing.

As we walked into the meeting, which had been in session for over one-and-a-half hours, every eye turned to us. I shall never forget the look on their faces as they beheld, for the first time in years, a representative of the General Authorities. It was not me, but the fact that a representative from headquarters had arrived—a time they'd all looked forward anxiously for during the long years of terrible war. (ETB Journal.)

The hall was filled beyond capacity, there being about 260 friends and members present, most of whom clearly reflected the stark horror and destruction through which they have passed. Yet their upturned faces shone forth with a warmth and appreciation that brought tears to our eyes.

This meeting in the Karlsruhe District of the West German Mission is the first meeting in the mission at which a member of the General Authorities has been in attendance since war began nearly seven years ago.

After the meeting we went to the door and shook hands with every person in attendance, and it was gratifying to see the look of faith and devotion that lighted their faces as they felt our warmth and sincere love for this people.

During the conference it was learned that many of our Saints have sustained great losses. Many are without adequate shelter, clothing, or food.

One family with two adopted children is living together in an unheated single room without water or cooking facilities. Nearly ninety percent of the city of Pforzheim, in which they formerly lived, was completely destroyed. Many of our members there were killed, and those who survived the annihilation bombings found themselves homeless and destitute.

During one night's bombing at Hamburg, twenty-seven of our members were killed, and on successive nights of bombing many more were either killed or rendered homeless.

The terrific bombardment of this country has destroyed the meetinghouses in all but a very few branches. Where no meeting halls are available, the Saints are doing their best to hold services in the homes of those members who were not bombed out.

The strain of inadequate housing, heating, food, and clothing is beginning to tell on our people. One of the critical problems that is being considered is that of trying to arrange some place for the many Saints to stay who are fleeing from the Russian Zone as refugees to Berlin. Reports were given that many are coming without food, without adequate clothing, and some trudging through the wintry snows barefooted.

Some of these refugees are dying in spite of all efforts being made on the part of the American-occupied zone to arrange wherever possible to house and feed these people. Being refugees, they are not permitted entrance into the other areas, and no arrangement is made for them to secure either food or clothing. Two projects for the temporary relief of Church members are being supervised by the mission headquarters in Berlin, but the large number of such refugees is making these facilities woefully inadequate.

We were caused to marvel at the devotion and faith of these good people. More members than ever before are paying their tithes and offerings and taking advantage of every means of association that is afforded by the Church. All the branches and districts are doing their utmost to care not only for themselves but for their brethren as well.

Last Friday a baptism was held in Bielefeld at which eleven new members entered the waters of baptism. It was necessary to cut a large hole through the ice on the river to serve as a baptismal font. Eleven other members were baptized the following night in Karlsruhe. The work throughout the mission seems to be well organized in spite of the difficulties, and the spiritual and financial condition of the mission is very good. (European Mission History.)

As we discussed with their leaders the problems before them, we felt no spirit of bitterness whatever, only a spirit of love and the reference frequently to their fellow members in the Berlin area whom they reported to be in much worse condition than those in the district they represented. Everywhere there was a spirit of cooperation as we mingled with these hungry, poorly clothed, and cold people. (European Mission History.)

My apron and handkerchief are wet with tears of appreciation for you as I write this letter.

I am watching the finances extremely carefully, and everything is all right.

I have the car checked and have the man always check as to when I should lubricate the car. I have three hundred more miles to go before a lubrication.

You know we are always thinking and praying for you, dearest, and hundreds of your dear friends and loved ones are doing the same. Many call me and tell me they are praying for you personally, not just with the whole.

Wouldn't you like me to send you some tuna fish, sugar, etc.? I am sending you some candy and nuts, and I'll try and make you some better cookies than the ones I have already sent you and pack them better. Tell me what you would like sent.

I would be happy to receive the two recipes and give you my lemon pie recipe:

Lemon pie filling: Grate outside of the rind of two lemons. Add to it three cups white sugar, two real large tablespoons white flour, and two real large tablespoons cornstarch.

Mix this together and then add yolks of five eggs. Add the juice of the two lemons and four cups of water. Stir constantly the minute the mixture is put on the stove.

Stir until the mixture has thickened and remove from stove.

Use the five egg whites for top of pie. Beat the whites stiff and add two or three tablespoons of sugar.

T, I imagine she knows how to make pie crust. Shall I send you my pie crust recipe?

The Lord is constantly blessing our efforts. If we do our part, the Lord never fails us. I feel His constant care over me continually.

May you have peace of mind always, T, and know that things are going well with us—and don't worry about us. We miss you greatly, but it shall bring its blessings. (FAB to ETB.)

MONDAY, MARCH 11, 1946:
KARLSRUHE, GERMANY

We visited with the Saints, met with the leaders, and consulted regarding the purchase of a building. I heard

43

Max Zimmer, President Benson, and Captain Badger tour Karlsruhe, Germany.

not one word of criticism pertaining to anything relating to the present conditions under which they are trying their best.

One could ask for no greater evidence of the power and blessings of the gospel in the lives of men and women than that which was shown by these devoted, but destitute, members of the Church. I believe this was the first time in my life that I had ever seen any of our members truly hungry and poorly clothed and living in a cold area without any heat in the building. (ETB to FAB.)

Attended a party in honor of President and Sister James L. Barker, who will be presiding over the French Mission. They will see my husband soon, and I told them to tell him I love him more every day and am always praying for him. (FAB Journal.)

TUESDAY, MARCH 12, 1946:
BASEL AND BERN, SWITZERLAND

We are doing everything in our power to get permission to send commodities into the occupied areas, even if we have to purchase some items here in Switzerland to take care of their immediate needs. To date this permission has not been granted. We are working with the International Red Cross today and also with officials of the Swiss government and the military authorities. (European Mission History.)

I sent three packages to London to my darling husband — candy, tuna fish, figs, cake, and pears. (FAB Journal.)

Wednesday, March 13, 1946:
Basel, Switzerland

I am most hopeful we can arrange to purchase immediately food and clothing in Switzerland to be trucked to the Berlin area to relieve the distress of our refugee Saints arriving in numbers from Poland and the Russian Zone. If this can be done, it will help to tide them over until we can arrange for shipments from home.

Food seems plentiful in Switzerland, but very few items are declared in surplus. It is not possible to buy rationed items, and most food items are rationed.

Received lovely and encouraging letters from my devoted and loyal wife and children. May the Lord bless them. (ETB Journal.)

I feel very keenly the great responsibility which is mine as we face the grave problems which confront our people in many of the European countries. I am not in the least discouraged. The Lord is blessing our efforts even beyond my fondest expectations. I know it is His purpose to take care of His Saints and have every confidence that He will open the way if we will do our part. We are striving to be worthy of His blessings.

May the Lord ever bless and comfort our Saints. My heart goes out to them. I love them dearly and would do anything within my power to relieve them. (ETB to FAB.)

Thursday, March 14, 1946:
Basel, Switzerland

Am happy and grateful tonight because the Lord has opened the way for us to get relief to our suffering Saints in the military areas.

The International Red Cross at Geneva has agreed to supervise the movement of our supplies into the occupied areas. By special arrangement they have also agreed to buy 10,000 Swiss francs of food, clothing, and bedding for immediate delivery to our people in the Berlin area. We gave authorization for this purchase and shipment at once and cabled the First Presidency to rush shipments to the occupied areas through the port at Antwerp.

Have written many letters today in preparation for an extended trip into the occupied areas. Received letters today from four of my children. (ETB Journal.)

Beth started taking cold and coughed a great deal. (FAB Journal.)

Friday, March 15, 1946:
Basel, Switzerland, and Frankfurt, Germany

Drove to Frankfurt, Germany, today from Basel. (ETB Journal.)

Along the way we went through several cities in which we have branches. As we were nearing Heidelberg, we passed a large number of men, women, and children at the city dumpgrounds frantically searching through refuse and garbage being unloaded from army trucks. We learned that this scavenger process is being repeated in all parts of the country due to the destitute condition of so many of the people.

Just a few miles farther on, we entered the beautiful city of Heidelberg, spared from bombing as an open hospital city. To see a large German city that looks livable and beautiful instead of presenting a depressing scene of ghastly ruins, twisted steel, and rubble was a most welcome sight. Here we met with some of the servicemen who are still stationed in this vicinity.

The remainder of our trip into Frankfurt took us through city after city that appeared to be sixty to eighty-five percent bombed out. The city of Darmstadt, in which we formerly had a thriving branch, is almost totally devastated. We learned later that with few exceptions our meeting halls have been completely destroyed and that between eighty and ninety percent of our members have been bombed out of their homes. Many valuable records, together with nearly every piece of branch and district furniture, have either been looted, confiscated, or destroyed through war damage. (European Mission History.)

We stopped at Freiburg to greet the Saints of that branch who were assembled in the small rented hall where they had been waiting for three hours in the hope they'd be able to see us as I had promised to stop at the home of a member long enough to bless their little baby.

We sang two hymns, had prayer, blessed the baby, and then I spoke to the eager Saints briefly.

Later I administered to a faithful brother in ill health who had been a French prisoner for three years and didn't know whether his wife and three daughters whom he left in eastern Germany were alive or dead.

We arrived at Frankfurt and were greeted warmly by LDS servicemen. (ETB Journal.)

Today I immediately put Beth to bed and plastered her, etc. I guess Beth caught the cold, and I have been overworking in trying to have people to the home too much. (FAB Journal.)

SATURDAY, MARCH 16, 1946:
FRANKFURT, GERMANY

Our first interview with General [Joseph T.] McNarney, the top general in the American forces, was in the I. G.

Throughout Germany, as here in Frankfurt, President Benson found cities reduced to rubble.

Farben Building in Frankfurt, which had been spared by "pin bombing" because the Americans expected it would be their headquarters when the war was over, and it was.

We had driven our little jeep up to the building, parked it, and gone in to see if we could get an appointment with the general. We wanted to get permission from him to make distribution of our welfare supplies to our own people through our own channels. Everything was being distributed through the military.

We were told by the colonel at the desk that we couldn't get an appointment for three days. The general was very busy with important delegations coming to see him.

We returned to our car and had a prayer together, then we went back in.

In the meantime the secretary at the desk had been changed, and in less than fifteen minutes we were in the presence of General McNarney.

Then I saw the Spirit operate on that man. I heard him say, "Under no conditions can you have permission to distribute your own supplies to your own people. They must come through the military."

Of course we recognized immediately that if we had to go through the military, our Saints wouldn't get much of the supplies, and so we started telling him about the program of the Church.

When he saw we were somewhat determined, he said, "Well, you go ahead and collect your supplies, and probably by the time you get them collected the policy will be changed."

I said, "General, they are already collected; they are always collected. We have ninety warehouses full of supplies. Within twenty-four hours from the time I wire our First Presidency in Salt Lake City, carloads of food, bedding, clothing, and medical supplies will be moving toward Germany."

When I said this, he said, "I never heard of people with such vision."

And before we left him we had written authorization to make our own distribution to our own people through our own channels, and from that moment on we had wonderful cooperation. (ETB Reminiscences.)

Permission was given to utilize the Red Cross facilities for transporting relief supplies to our Saints.

In regard to a proposed program for sending starved and undernourished children from Germany to Switzerland for brief vacations and special care, we were informed that final permission of the Swiss government and the International Red Cross, together with full permission from General Clay in Berlin, would have to be secured.

Permission to continue our projected travels was granted and a letter of introduction to General Lucius Clay from General McNarney prepared. (European Mission History.)

My doctor was out of town, so I worked hard with Beth.

49

When I did get the doctor, he said I had taken care of her very well and had done all I could have done. He found she had pneumonia. He had her take sulfa drug, and I've worked hard night and day. (FAB Journal.)

SUNDAY, MARCH 17, 1946:
FRANKFURT, GERMANY

This has been a heavy but joyful day. We have held meetings all day with officers and Saints. We have also visited and eaten meager meals with them, partly provided by the servicemen. Two hundred thirty-seven poorly clothed, ill fed, but faithful Saints were at the service held in a partly bombed-out university auditorium. The Spirit of the Lord was present in power, and in the two-and-one-half-hour meeting we were all lifted far above the mundane things of the world. We took photos of the group of refugees and the entire meeting. (ETB Journal.)

Reports given revealed that eighty-two members were killed during the war while serving in the armed forces, seventy-one civilians were killed through bombings and shellfire, and approximately fifteen hundred have not yet been accounted for. Between eighty and eighty-five percent of the membership of the mission have been bombed out of their homes, necessitating their removal into the country area round about. This scattered condition of our people presents a great obstacle in attendance at meetings or participation in Church activities. Most branches are meeting in the homes of members until they can secure some type of quarters as a permanent meeting place.

Further, it was learned that the Saints in the French Zone have very great need for assistance. In this zone particularly nearly all animals have been confiscated by the French government. Potato peelings are selling for twenty-five dollars per hundred pounds, while on the "black market" people can buy one hundred pounds of potatoes for one package of American cigarettes. Cases were reported where an entire ton of potatoes was purchased for one carton of cigarettes and a few cents.

During and since the war the branch and district Relief Societies have cooperated with the presiding brethren in organizing welfare projects and caring for the homeless families and returning servicemen. As bombings became more intense and the number of homeless and destitute grew to mammoth proportions, the amount of assistance rendered was of necessity reduced; however, they have been able to assist greatly with the refugees and displaced persons arriving.

During the Relief Society centennial celebration in 1942, fifty branches had organized societies and a missionwide pageant, written by one of their number (a nationally known poetess), was presented with gratifying success. Since that time the blackout restrictions, intensified bombings, and subsequent loss of homes and meeting places have reduced the number of active units to half the original number. As rapidly as possible places to meet are being secured and they are organizing themselves to assist in the distribution of Church welfare supplies to the stricken families. (European Mission History.)

In spite of repeated bombings which destroyed buildings on all sides, the mission home has remained in livable condition. At one time three 1,000-pound bombs fell in front of the mission home. Their failure to explode saved the building from being totally destroyed. Most of the damage present resulted through the dynamiting of the bridges across the river by the retreating armies. The bridge in front of the mission home required eight charges of dynamite and bombs to render it impassable.

Sister Ilse Bruenger Foerster, who has served as mission secretary since the outbreak of war, had to undergo ruthless examinations by the Gestapo on the charge that she was sending mission funds to America. After two weeks of grueling examinations and constant surveillance, during which nearly all mission records were either burned or confiscated, she was released with the threat that not only her life but the life of all of her family and relatives would be blotted out if any result of the questioning were ever revealed.

During this critical time she was expecting her first child, but in spite of threats and the terrific strain exerted upon her, she denied every charge and refuted every accusation—so much so that they were caused to marvel at her intense faith and devotion to the Church.

Recently three German prisoners of war, who had just been released from a prisoner of war camp near Ogden, Utah, entered the local employment placement agency where Sister Foerster is employed as a translator. One of these men was a former doctor, another a former dentist, and the third a former architect. While filling out the questionnaires, they passed out tracts and books to the employees. Then they addressed the group, declaring they had received these while in the prison camp in America and that they felt they had at last found the truth and the only Church upon the face of the earth, for they had not only studied and learned of its teaching but they had seen the wonderful results in the lives of the members of said church. They felt an obligation to tell others of the great happiness that had come into their lives. The tracts they had passed out were Mormon tracts and the books were copies of the Book of Mormon. This is only one of many faith-promoting experiences that have been related to us. (European Mission History.)

I was so thrilled when President Clark called and said they had received a cable from you and that you were in Basel, Switzerland. He said you were doing a marvelous work. You certainly are accomplishing things in a hurry. I know you well enough that I could expect that from you. (FAB to ETB.)

One of Barbara's friends said, "Won't your daddy be home

*for Christmas?" Barbara said, "I don't know. We just hope so."
And her little friend said, "If he can work both day and night,
maybe he will be able to come home sooner." (FAB to ETB.)*

*I sent you three boxes of things last week—first, a box of
tuna fish, pears, and nuts; second, fruit cake, nuts, and figs (I
am sorry the fruit cake isn't homemade. I was able to buy some
gum drops yesterday, so the next one will be homemade—gum
drop fruit cake.); third, twenty-four Hershey chocolate bars. Yesterday I sent you another two-pound box of Cummings chocolates.
Do you need sugar or anything in particular? Please let me know,
and I'll send what you need. I am never too busy to do it. (FAB
to ETB.)*

*I am quite tired but blessed and happy for what the Lord does
for me. I am greatly blessed—I have every blessing one could ask
for, but I feel a little tired tonight because the past three nights
the baby has been sick with a bad temperature and cold. But I
know she will be all right. (FAB to ETB.)*

MONDAY, MARCH 18, 1946:
FRANKFURT, GERMANY

Have spent the day in a continuation of our work contacting military and civil authorities regarding our work
and people in the American Zone. Secured permission
from civil authorities to bring in some thirty families from
eastern Germany and Poland from among our refugees.
(ETB Journal.)

*I have stayed close to the baby. Had Elder Spencer W. Kimball
administer to the baby. The Lord blessed her. (FAB Journal.)*

TUESDAY, MARCH 19, 1946:
FRANKFURT AND HANOVER, GERMANY

Bade our LDS servicemen, who have been so kind to
us here, good-bye and left for Hanover in the British Zone.
Our servicemen escorted us to the outskirts of the city.

We drove hard to try and make a meeting scheduled with five district presidents from the northern part of the West German Mission.

All along the way we noted the terrifying effects of the war, especially in cities with factories and railway yards. Most of the way we traveled on the famous autobahn and witnessed, to our sorrow, beautiful and costly bridges blown up by the retreating forces requiring often miles of detour.

The farming areas were lovely to behold, although most are short of manpower. We saw no tractors as these were destroyed by the retreating forces. Production, so desperately needed, will be reduced because of the shortages. However, these industrious rural people — old men and women mostly — seem to be doing their best with cows and steers used to supplement the few poor horses left.

In Hanover we saw a city in ruins. This, I believe, is the worst we have seen. It appears that not one building in the city proper is undamaged, and most buildings are leveled to the ground. To look up some of the streets with every building laid waste fills one's heart with a weird and sad feeling. People walking about in the ruins seem almost as though they were from another world.

My heart grows heavy and my eyes fill with tears as I picture in my mind's eyes these scenes of horror and destruction.

We met with the district presidents in a small half-bombed-out room on a second floor amid the ruins as we listened to their reports on conditions of the past war years. Our faith was strengthened as we listened to their reports of courageous activities. Although touched deeply, we were moved to thank the Lord for the gospel as it has been demonstrated in the lives of these faithful Saints. (ETB Journal.)

Reports indicated that Hamburg was almost completely destroyed. Where there were six branches, they now have only one, but are meeting together and have twenty-five local part-time missionaries and five full-time missionaries preaching the gospel.

All branch and district properties have been lost, including all books (personal as well as mission), all tracts, many of the records, reports, etc. Few sacrament dishes or glasses are available. This report was multiplied many-fold as each district reported. Every city in this part of the mission in which we had a branch has been seventy to ninety percent destroyed.

Only two families in Bremen retained their homes and both of these severely damaged. In other branches every member has lost his home. Some branches were deprived of all their priesthood members, resulting in some branches not having had the sacrament for over a year. In one case an entire funeral service was conducted by members of the Relief Society. (European Mission History.)

With only two hours' notice, we held a public meeting with about 175 Saints in a heatless, partially bombed-out schoolhouse still partly usable. The spirit of the meeting was marvelous to feel and behold.

How I longed for power to lift these good people from their heartrending state. We did all in our power to help them and offered such assistance as we could and promised them we'd see them again soon.

I retired tonight with a sad but thankful heart on a straw tick in three pieces with no linen of any sort and blankets and quarters filthy because of the lack of soap and water. (ETB Journal.)

President George Albert Smith, with his son-in-law, administered and blessed the baby. She has been real sick. He gave her a beautiful blessing.

I know the Lord blessed her because we were almost forced to take her to the hospital. But I know it was the administration

Enroute from Hanover to Berlin, President Benson and those traveling with him endured mechanical difficulties.

that made her keep a lower temperature. She is still very sick but is making progress.

Everyone has been kind. President Smith called. President Smith kissed all the girls on their foreheads and said that was in place of their daddy. President Smith placed Beth's name in the temple.

I received grand and beautiful letters from my devoted and loving husband from Basel, Switzerland, and Paris. (FAB Journal.)

Please don't worry about Beth, dear. I know the Lord will bless her to be well and strong again.

I have been trying to do too much, I guess, but I am very blessed and thankful I have you, the gospel, and the children. That means everything.

The baby has pneumonia, and we may have to take her to the hospital tonight. Pray for her, dear. (FAB to ETB.)

WEDNESDAY, MARCH 20, 1946:
HANOVER AND BERLIN, GERMANY

At daylight we left Hanover for Berlin, traveling along the autobahn through the Russian Zone, the only corridor

Many highways and bridges throughout Europe were impassable, such as the Reichsautobahn Bridge between Hanover and Berlin, making travel tedious.

upon which Americans are permitted to enter Berlin. The Lord opened the way, however, and although we were checked by British, Russian, and American military authorities, we were in each case permitted to proceed.

Guards, armed with bayonets, were stationed along the route about every five miles. We were permitted to pass safely through unmolested in spite of the many warnings and stories of danger passed on to us by the various military units.

We reached the American sector of the Berlin area safely after witnessing the results of war on every hand and were, after several hours' wait, finally taken to our quarters. (ETB Journal.)

The sight of Berlin is indescribable. Not a building has escaped damage, and miles of the city are laid in utter waste. It is a scene of shocking desolation. (European Mission History.)

It is impossible for one to describe adequately the tremendous changes that have taken place in this great land. The extent of bombing damage varies of course between cities; however, in many of the cities practically every building is damaged.

The job of taking care of our Saints, even as to their most meager needs, is overwhelming, and as we contemplate their rehabilitation, it becomes staggering. The Lord is blessing our efforts, and we feel sure His blessings will continue with us if we do our best. (European Mission History.)

Elder Harold B. Lee and Brother Alma Sonne called to see how the baby was. They administered to the baby. Brother Lee gave a beautiful prayer.

Our baby is being greatly blessed and is doing much better but still has to be watched carefully.

President J. Reuben Clark called.

Dozens and dozens are calling by phone and at home and bringing nice things to eat. We are very blessed to have such grand and devoted friends.

Apostle Lee read us a letter from our wonderful husband and father. (FAB Journal.)

Yesterday I told you our baby had pneumonia and would probably have to go to the hospital. I am happy to tell you today that she has made satisfactory improvement and it wasn't necessary to take her.

The Lord has surely blessed her. Everyone has just been marvelous. I didn't realize that we had so many kind and loving friends. (FAB to ETB.)

The Lord has surely given me added strength to carry on too. I have been up with her constantly for nights giving her sulfa drug and mustard plasters. I don't like anyone else to do it, and many a night I've held her in my arms all night. It doesn't seem I feel so tired either when morning comes, and many times I have felt the Lord, you, and Mother have been very close to me in helping me carry on. (FAB to ETB.)

When I get to bed at midnight, then I am praying for you, and I think you're just getting up in Europe and you're praying for me. The only difference is that I am going to bed and you're getting up, but we're both praying and thinking of each other at the same time.

I will still have to continue regularly the sulfa and plasters night and day for a while, but the doctor says she's over the danger line and with good care she'll be well.

I know that all will be well with her, and whatever comes or goes I feel will be right. If I am always living my religion and doing my part, the Lord will certainly do His.

The Lord is taking grand care of me, and there is no person more abundantly blessed and happier than I. (FAB to ETB.)

I have been given an abundance of added strength during Beth's sickness. I have felt His Spirit so close to me at times in protecting, directing, guiding, and comforting me that I have marveled at it. (FAB to ETB.)

There have been profiting experiences come from Beth's illness, such as the family following instructions better — working closer and more unitedly together — and I suppose it's taught me not to invite and have guests and folks out so much at the home. But I enjoy doing and helping others what little I can, and it's grand to be working and enjoying the results of the same. (FAB to ETB.)

President Clark has been grand to want to help, but I tell him I don't need anyone in to help me — that I'll get along all right. (FAB to ETB.)

You told of the little children you gave gum to, and how thrilled they were. I am sending you a box of gum and fruit candy drops. I think it would be so nice (as you have already discovered)

59

to carry some of this gum and candy around with you and give to the dear little Mormon children and others. (FAB to ETB.)

The baby is feeling so very much better. It's midnight and I must give her a mustard plaster. She is the sweetest little soul. (FAB to ETB.)

THURSDAY, MARCH 21, 1946:
BERLIN, GERMANY

Made two visits to the army dispensary in an effort to get relief from a sinus infection and some pain from neuralgia. Some relief resulted.

Drove through once beautiful Berlin. The wreckage to lovely government buildings, universities, monuments, museums, parks, and business blocks cannot possibly be understood unless seen. My soul rebels as I attempt to describe it.

My heart is heavy as I reflect on these awful, never-to-be-forgotten scenes. Truly war is hell in all its fury. (ETB Journal.)

One sister came to the house with her apron and wanted to spend the day helping me in the home, and another sister also came to the home and wanted to help me. But I told them I wouldn't need them — all I wanted was their faith and prayers to bless our baby so she would get well.

The baby is doing very nicely. She is making a speedy recovery.

The General Authorities and Quorum of Twelve have been very kind to remember the baby with their faith and prayers. I know that it was the prayers that were raised up in the baby's behalf and the power of the priesthood that have made her get well again so speedy. We have also had a very kind and good doctor. (FAB Journal.)

FRIDAY, MARCH 22, 1946:
BERLIN, GERMANY

Continued conferences with military government officials most of the day and held long meeting with the acting mission presidency.

Had a most satisfactory conference with General Lucius D. Clay, U.S. Deputy Governor for Germany. Our group was assured of his full cooperation, and we received his appreciation that the Church was on the job in the occupied areas ready to help in the mammoth work of rehabilitation.

The general approved the resumption of our pre-war Church program, including MIA activities and the organization of Boy Scout work.

We also discussed with the general the question of transportation of Church literature, purchase of automobiles, unfreezing of Church funds, and the resumption of normal missionary activities. In all of these matters, he expressed sympathy and assured us of his support, but urged that we be patient and not expect too much during the next two months. (European Mission History.)

In 1938 and 1939 the Genealogical Society of Utah tried to make arrangements for buying microfilms of genealogical records from the German government without success. After the missionaries were evacuated, Brother Paul Langheinrich, first counselor to the acting mission president and mission genealogical leader, made arrangements for the German government to construct a microfilming machine for use of the Church. The machine was finished, but war between Germany and the USA began, terminating further work.

Brother Langheinrich watched developments closely, and after war had ceased he wrote a letter to the commander-in-chief of the Russian occupation forces, asking for permission to provide foodstuffs for our suffering refugee Saints and also for permission to search for and receive title to all genealogical records and film in this territory to become property of the Genealogical Society and the Church.

Full permission was granted in both cases and, after long searching for these hidden records, a large group was found in an old mineshaft hidden in the mountains of Thuringer Forest.

The first discovery netted six to seven thousand church books, photo copies of most of these books, and some 5,000 films. This carload of records is now in the mission office.

Two days ago a much larger store was found in another mine — nearly three carloads — among which are over 140 boxes of microfilms from church books, 15,000 photo copies of books, etc., which will contain possibly more than 100,000,000 names. They will weigh about twenty-five tons. These materials, on the basis of the permission granted by the Russian government, became property of our Church with certain reservations. Permission is now being secured to move these to the Church offices.

A very vigorous missionary program has been undertaken by this mission. They now have twenty-one full-time missionaries working in all parts of the Russian military zone, four lady missionaries working full-time in the mission office, and six more brethren being called to also work as full-time missionaries.

Present conditions in this mission make it impossible to send missionaries from Zion inasmuch as the entire mission is in the Russian Zone of occupation. Local missionaries, however, have been well received and are able to pursue their missionary activities almost unhindered.

All of our branches and districts in the areas now occupied by Poland are closed to any missionary work, and all Germans in these areas are being deported as refugees primarily to the British Zone of occupation. The Germans in Czechoslovakia likewise are being deported to the American Zone. Most of our Saints in this area have either fled, died, or are living under most shocking discomforting conditions.

In spite of receiving no rations as refugees for nearly five months and arriving without bedding or clothing beyond that which they were wearing, the Saints organized local welfare groups and were not only successful in caring for their immediate clothing and subsistence needs, but were also able to work cooperatively together in securing work and homes for the able-bodied families so they might move out and become self-supporting. Those remaining in the temporary refugee quarters were required to work in the branches and districts among the members and received work receipts which served as a basis for their receiving needed assistance. The future is very critical, however, inasmuch as all the members have shared every available item, and they now are faced with very urgent needs.

As nearly as can be determined, 184 Church members were killed in the war and an additional 120 died of bombings, disease, and starvation—making a total of 304. Starvation is very near to many of our people, and all the help we can give them will not come too soon. In the mission 1,728 members are still unaccounted for. What has happened to them is still unknown. (European Mission History.)

Brother and Sister Marion Romney called and brought me a lovely cake. (FAB Journal.)

SATURDAY, MARCH 23, 1946:
BERLIN, GERMANY

The testimonies of the Lord's guidance and protection during the war years were as great [in Berlin] as any in the Church. Many instances were related in which the inspiration and direction of our Heavenly Father enabled the mission leaders to inspire their associates to greater faith and activity. Never have greater faith and activity been known in this mission. Financially as well as spiritually the mission is in very fine condition.

Many new friends who are genuinely interested in the gospel are meeting in homes or bombed-out buildings to hear the message of the gospel.

Almost without exception the branches have all been bombed out and have lost their entire possessions. Every effort is being made to rent, rebuild, or buy suitable buildings or halls in which the members and their friends may meet and in which the entire program of the Church may be carried out. (European Mission History.)

We visited the completely demolished building where our mission headquarters used to be. The office force and missionaries went over to the rented home of Brother Langheinrich the night before the bombing on his recommendation, otherwise they would all have been killed as the building was completely ruined. (ETB Journal.)

SUNDAY, MARCH 24, 1946:
BERLIN, GERMANY

This has been a glorious day with much joy and a few periods of deep sadness. As we rode to visit our five Sunday Schools and to attend the meeting, I witnessed scenes that seemed almost outside this world.

The worst destruction I have witnessed was seen today. I stood in the wreckage that once was the proud headquarters of the Hitler government, including Hitler's office, private living quarters, ball and reception rooms, and finally the underground fortress where he spent his last hours during the terrible siege of Berlin.

I saw the pomp and beauty of once proud Berlin, at one time heralded by godless leaders as the product of the "master race" that would throw the principles of Christianity out the window and conquer the world by force, now a mass of sad wreckage — that which had taken 1,000 years to build completely destroyed, as it were, in a day.

64

As I rode through the streets and walked through some impassable by auto, I smelled the odor of decaying human bodies, saw half-starved women paying exorbitant prices anxiously for potato peelings.

I saw soldiers forcefully breaking up a flourishing black market where cigarettes were the principal medium of exchange.

I saw old men and women with small hatchets eagerly digging at tree stumps and roots in an effort to get scraps of fuel and then pulling those home for miles on anything that would roll—from two little wheels of a once baby carriage to small wagons—as beasts of burden.

Later I faced in a cold half-wrecked third floor auditorium off a bombed street 480 cold half-starved but faithful Latter-day Saints in a conference meeting. It was an inspiration to see the light of faith and hear their harrowing experiences, including murder, rape, and starvation of their loved ones. Yet there was no bitterness or anger but a sweet reciprocation and expression of faith in the gospel. We were together in a partly bombed building for three-and-a-half hours. (ETB Journal.)

Not a single member registered any complaint about their circumstances in spite of the fact that some were in the last stages of starvation right before our very eyes.

In Berlin alone we were told that there are well over one hundred suicides daily due to the mental attitude of the people who have no hope in view of the ravages of war. Our Saints, on the other hand, are full of hope, courage, and faith, and everywhere they look cheerfully forward with expressions of deepest faith for the gospel and for their membership in the Church. It was one of the greatest demonstrations we have ever seen of the real fruits of the gospel in the lives of men and women.

Our travels during the day to the various meetings took us through mile after mile of unspeakable destruction and desolation. Words cannot begin to describe the ruin that

65

People in Heidelberg, Germany, rummage through the garbage looking for scraps of food.

has been heaped upon this city. Only one small portion of the front wall of the former East German Mission home remains standing. Across the street where the once beautiful Tiergarten stood is nothing but a yawning wilderness of splintered tree stumps and an occasional badly shattered lifeless tree. Many streets are still impassable, piled high with rubble.

Hardly a day passes that skeletonized buildings do not crash into the street below, often burying passersby. Most bridges are entirely blown up, and the large mass of unsupported, shell-ridden walls presents a constant menace as they continue to crumble and cave in. Traveling amid such surroundings leaves one with a feeling so appalling that it must be experienced to be understood. (European Mission History.)

Elder and Sister Harold B. Lee brought a real large beautiful bunch of daffodil flowers to the family. (FAB Journal.)

The destroyed Kaiserhof Hotel in Berlin is typical of the destruction found throughout that city.

MONDAY, MARCH 25, 1946:
BERLIN AND NUREMBERG, GERMANY

Left Berlin for Nuremberg. There was no place to get meals enroute as no restaurants or cafes are operating. We were able to get some K-rations, which we ate for lunch and dinner as we rode, having missed breakfast.

We drove by way of Helmstedt, Kassel, and Bamberg in order to avoid the regular Russian area. For fourteen hours we drove, detouring for bombed-out bridges, and reached Nuremberg, the scene of the present trials of German war criminals. (ETB Journal.)

What a sight it was to see nearly 200 shivering Saints assembled in a badly damaged classroom of a former schoolhouse. They had begun meeting at 7:30 P.M. and continued to remain waiting our arrival in spite of the fact that the military curfew necessitated their remaining in the room overnight instead of returning to their homes. After the meeting they stretched out on the cold floor, huddled together in groups, to rest for the night. We were caused to marvel at their faith and devotion! (European Mission History.)

After visiting among and blessing some of them, we went to the partly destroyed hotel where the officials of the trials are staying. Half of the building is destroyed, and we walked through halls of rubble to get to our cold and bare quarters. We were most thankful for an army cot with clean linen. (ETB Journal.)

The old city of Nuremberg is accredited by many to be the worst bombed section in Germany. Not a single building remains standing and many of the streets are still hopelessly blocked with rubble and bomb craters. Both of our meetinghouses are completely destroyed. Nearly every member was bombed or burned out of their homes one or more times. The present need for relief and assistance here, as in most other sections we have visited, is very great. Every possible effort to help is being considered by the local Saints and they are doing a remarkable job, but their resources are now exhausted. (European Mission History.)

TUESDAY, MARCH 26, 1946:
NUREMBERG, GERMANY, AND PRAGUE, CZECHOSLO-VAKIA

Arose early and inspected a bomb-damaged half-house which the local Nuremberg Branch proposed to purchase. Left for Prague, Czechoslovakia. (ETB Journal.)

The sight of entering Czechoslovakia and seeing most cities without serious damage — to see the shop windows filled and attractively decorated, to see the factory chimneys smoking and people cheerfully working — was a real treat after having seen nothing but desolation and despair for over a week. It seemed almost like entering another world.

President Benson and escorts stop outside of what had been Hitler's private bunker in Berlin.

As we entered Prague, the city lights were twinkling. We had little difficulty finding the mission home and were warmly welcomed by Elder Josef Roubicek, acting mission president, and his family.

Nearly all of the 115 members of the Czechoslovakia Mission have remained active and faithful to the Church. Through their combined efforts, they have been able to remain self-supporting as a mission in spite of their small number.

Most of the mission funds have been "frozen" in the banks until a restabilization policy can be effected, and in spite of their having less than five dollars in accessible funds, they are carrying on a vigorous campaign of missionary proselyting work.

A strict system of rationing is in effect, and many items are still impossible to secure. As a result, the welfare packages the Saints have received have been most welcome and have filled a real need, a need which continues. (European Mission History.)

President George Albert Smith called on me this evening. (FAB Journal.)

WEDNESDAY, MARCH 27, 1946:
PRAGUE AND PILSEN, CZECHOSLOVAKIA

Called on the Lord Mayor of Prague and on the American Ambassador and the first secretary. Held a fine meeting with twenty-seven Saints and blessed two babies. (ETB Journal.)

Permission was granted for missionaries and a mission president from Zion to resume their proselyting activities in this land. The Church enjoys a very favorable reputation. Before leaving for Vienna later in the afternoon a special meeting was held with the Saints, 29 attending, and an unusually sweet spirit enjoyed. (European Mission History.)

On the way to Prague yesterday, we had tire trouble, and three more flat tires in rapid succession this evening made us alter our plans of trying to drive through to Linz, Austria. We stopped overnight in Pilsen, Czechoslovakia, where we were able to secure good vulcanizing service. (European Mission History.)

I feel so much better today. I can now carry on in "full blast." That spark the Lord has given me must not become dim — it's a priceless blessing and possession.

Friends and neighbors have been so kind to me. Many have called today, among them are Elder George F. Richards and Sister David O. McKay.

The baby and I had a much better night. (FAB to ETB.)

THURSDAY, MARCH 28, 1946:
PILSEN, CZECHOSLOVAKIA, AND VIENNA, AUSTRIA

Left Pilsen after repairing tires and rode hard all day to Vienna via Passau and Linz. Roads were rough and

President Benson poses with a group of Saints in Prague, Czechoslovakia.

bridges out, necessitating long detours, but we arrived in Vienna to find a hall full of Saints and friends who had been awaiting our arrival for two hours. We met with these faithful souls for an hour and then with the district presidency and the branch presidents of Austria for one-and-a-half hours.

I am grateful that this day we have had the way opened for us and that in all our travel we moved unmolested in spite of serious warnings given by friends and officials who seemed sincerely interested in our welfare. Guards with rifles and tommy guns stopped us many times, but each time we were permitted to proceed. (ETB Journal.)

President Smith dropped in to see me and got me out of bed last night.

President Clark had given me quite a scolding about working so hard and to see that I got enough rest to carry on, so I repented and went to bed at nine o'clock—and who should get me up but President Smith calling. (FAB to ETB.)

His visit to Dachau was one of President Benson's most sobering experiences.

SATURDAY, MARCH 30, 1946:
MUNICH AND STUTTGART, GERMANY

It is two months today since we left Salt Lake City by plane for Europe in accordance with my appointment to preside over the European Mission and look after the relief needs of our people and reestablish our work again in these war-torn countries. As I contemplate our unusual accomplishments, my heart is filled with gratitude to God for His blessing in opening the way and sustaining us with His loving care.

Two months ago no one, I am sure, even dreamed so much would be done in so short a time. There is so much to be accomplished, and the needs are so great that with all my heart I pray for a continuance of His sustaining power in the mission to which He has called us. (ETB Journal.)

We stopped at Dachau to visit the concentration camp

President Benson, Max Zimmer, and Fred Babbel inspect the rows of U.S. howitzers left behind at Dachau.

there. The things we saw and the statistics which were given us made us shudder to realize how far men will go in the direction of evil and sin when they fail to accept the eternal truths of the gospel.

We visited the human crematories, saw the gallows, the trenches in which innocent victims were machine-gunned, and the kennels in which prisoners were thrown to be torn to pieces by the ferocious dogs kept there. In this camp alone over 238,000 persons were exterminated. Some of the ashes of the victims were sent to their near relatives, who were required to pay a stipulated sum for them or suffer themselves in turn to be subjected to the horrors of such a camp.

Persons were thus systematically and brutally killed in this and the other some 300 such camps established by the Nazis. The fiendish bestiality that was here related to us made us sick at heart.

Today over 20,000 S.S. troops are confined in the prison

barracks awaiting trial at the conclusion of the major war criminals trials being held in Nuremberg.

Later President Max Zimmer related how plans were discovered in the German Embassy in Switzerland, after the cessation of hostilities in May, for the construction of five such concentration camps in Switzerland by the Nazis after their planned seizure of that land. German troops were at the borders for the intended invasion, but the heavy losses and unexpected reverses at Stalingrad necessitated redeploying the troops at the Swiss border, and thus the invasion of that land was averted. The names of several of our Swiss members were found to be on the list of those intended to be sent to these camps, so it is with gratitude in their hearts that our Swiss Saints thank the Lord for having spared their land.

From here we went to Stuttgart, where announcements were made over the radio of our meeting with the Saints this evening. We were gratified to see 275 persons in attendance of which at least 100 were investigators and 16 were servicemen.

In this meeting President Max Zimmer, Chaplain Howard C. Badger, Brother Frederick W. Babbel, and I sang "Let the Lower Lights Be Burning," to the delight of the entire audience. On our trip we have often sung the songs of Zion together and decided to make a public appearance before becoming separated. We named our quartet "The K-Ration Quartet." (European Mission History.)

SUNDAY, MARCH 31, 1946:
STUTTGART, GERMANY, AND BASEL, SWITZERLAND

Left Stuttgart and arrived in Basel. Spent balance of day reading mail forwarded from London. Received the shocking news that my youngest child (nineteen months) was critically ill with pneumonia.

After devout prayer, I placed a call from Basel, Switzerland, to my wife in Salt Lake City. In minutes I heard her sweet voice and received the assurance that the baby

The "K-Ration Quartet," composed of Max Zimmer, President Benson, Fred Babbel and Chaplain Badger, perform in Stuttgart, Germany.

is well on the way to recovery, for which I thank the Lord. I also thank Him for the wonders of science which make, through His inspiration, the telephone possible. (ETB Journal.)

I arrived at Basel just about two hours before it was time to dedicate the new Basel chapel.

We often received mail there, and there was a letter from Flora. I opened it hurriedly and learned for the first time that Beth had been critically ill with pneumonia. The letter was several days old because we had been traveling. It was a great shock.

I went immediately to my knees in prayer and then placed a call for Flora in Salt Lake. It usually took from one to three days to get a call through. As I placed the call, I went to my knees again in prayer, asking that the Lord would open the way. It was less than fifteen minutes from the time I placed the call until I was talking with Flora through a perfect connection.

I was greatly relieved to hear her say that Beth was well on her way to recovery. She had been administered to by President George Albert Smith and some of the other brethren, following which she took a turn for the better.

I was greatly relieved and thankful to the Lord and went to the dedication with increased appreciation for the priesthood and the faith and care of a devoted wife and family. (ETB Reminiscences.)

This day shall never be forgotten because my loving husband called me long distance over the telephone from Basel, Switzerland. I am indeed thankful for him and hope the Lord to bless him constantly because he is so anxious to do good upon this earth.

Our baby, dear little Flora Beth, is over the pneumonia. (FAB Journal.)

MONDAY, APRIL 1, 1946:
BASEL, SWITZERLAND

Dictating letters and attending to mission business all day in Basel. (ETB Journal.)

You can never know how happy and thrilled and soul-satisfying it made me feel when I heard your sweet and loving voice over the telephone. (FAB to ETB.)

The baby is over her pneumonia but is left very weak and very much underweight. I am feeding her an egg yolk in each bottle of milk she takes, and she just loves it. I am sure this will help to build her up. The sulfa drug is hard on their little bodies, but I know she will do all right. I am giving her close care, and the Lord is constantly with me. She has been off her feet for about three weeks now, but she eats well and is happy and sweeter every day.

I knew without a doubt that the Lord would make her well and strong again, and it didn't seem to hurt my body to stay up countless nights and plaster her every two hours day and night and hold her close to my body and rock her sweet little precious body close to mine.

Many asked me if I wasn't afraid being alone when she was so sick. I told them I wasn't alone or afraid in the least. The Lord and His angels were constantly helping and working with me. I could just feel them, and I was so happy and peaceful when I worked over the little soul.

In the morning, as day broke, I never felt tired and I could carry on my day's work just as though I had a good night's rest.

His angels were actually helping take care of our baby and helping me with the work. I don't know how it was all accomplished so well and her speedy recovery came so fast if it hadn't been for the Lord's help and the many prayers for her recovery and the thoughtful things folks did and said.

We knew that your prayers were offered up in her behalf, and that you, as her loving father, always would be praying for her health and well-being. Your prayers helped so much, dearest. I know that you are constantly praying for me and our little flock of children. I can feel it so much, and I couldn't carry on without your faith, love, and devotion for us. (FAB to ETB.)

The tasks which have been given to you and me are not beyond our strength, "T", its pangs and toils are not beyond our endurance as long as we have faith in each other, live our religion, pray always, and have willpower to direct our thoughts and energies along the proper channels. (FAB to ETB.)

TUESDAY, APRIL 2, 1946:
BASEL AND BERN, SWITZERLAND

Left Basel for Bern. After transacting some business here, we rode up to Interlaken and Grindelwald for a view of the soul-inspiring Alps. Then we drove to Neuchatel, where we held a splendid meeting with the Saints in the Swiss district of the French Mission. Members were present from all of the four branches. (ETB Journal.)

After traveling several weeks in a land that leaves one

77

appalled and sick at heart to witness the terrible scenes of destruction and poverty everywhere, this was a most delightful and restful change. (European Mission History.)

President J. Reuben Clark called on me for a few minutes. President Clark said I deserved a rest. (FAB Journal.)

FRIDAY, APRIL 5, 1946:
PARIS, FRANCE, AND LIEGE, BELGIUM

Along much of our journey from Paris to Liege, Belgium, we passed through mile after mile of stores of munitions sheltered under corrugated steel shelters. These concentrated ammunition stores, which were in evidence most of the way to the Belgium border, along with occasional burned out tanks, destroyed trucks, cars, etc., were practically the only remaining signs of the war just ended. (European Mission History.)

In a special meeting held in Liege with Elder Paul Devignez, acting president, and his counselors it was learned that over 600 welfare packages have been received by the Saints. All packages have been opened upon entering the country, and some items have been removed by marauders, but these packages have been set aside by the members for shipment to the Saints in Germany as soon as permission to do so is forthcoming. Such unselfishness is most commendable.

Among a people in such great need, it was an inspiration to see that their anxiety for their brethren and sisters in Germany exceeded their concern for themselves. Foodstuffs, especially fats, vitamins, milk, and cereals for children, are still urgently needed. It was reported reliably that approximately one-third of all the children are afflicted with tuberculosis as a result of malnutrition. (European Mission History.)

This is the first day of general conference in Salt Lake.

My thoughts have turned westward many times today as I realize I'm missing a general conference of the Church for the first time in many years. I am fully contented, however, and happy and grateful to be here where I'm sure the Lord wants me to be. I thank Him for every blessing. (ETB Journal.)

Attended April conference — the first session. All the General Authorities were present except our dear and beloved husband and Apostle Cowley, who was ill. (FAB Journal.)

I attended the opening session of conference. I enjoyed it so much and was indeed happy to be able to go. I thought and prayed for you much, as many hundreds of others were doing for you. (FAB to ETB.)

I surely thrill with pride and joy over the marvelous work you are doing with the Lord's help. I know the Lord is surely close to you at all times, and I know you are working extremely hard with the Lord with no fear or doubt in your mind at any time, knowing always that right shall prevail and that insurmountable things can and will be accomplished by you and the Lord.

Your faith is undaunted and never wavers but is always firm, knowing that you shall succeed in all righteous things and that truth shall prevail. (FAB to ETB.)

SATURDAY, APRIL 6, 1946:
LIEGE AND ANTWERP, BELGIUM

It is 116 years today since, in the goodness of the Lord, His Church was again organized on the earth. How grateful I am that I have been made a partaker of its rich blessings.

The more I see of the world, the more I am convinced that it needs the blessings of the restored gospel. I hope and pray that we may all do our utmost to carry it to the children of men and that God will touch the hearts of people everywhere that they may see the beauties of the gospel. We left Liege for Antwerp and Amsterdam. The countryside was lovely, especially in Holland where we saw the first of the fields of tulips and daffodils on every side. (ETB Journal.)

Listened to an inspiring conference. We surely miss our father and husband. The first conference he hasn't been able to attend since being an apostle. (FAB Journal.)

President Clark and his daughter called on me. They were so thrilled and happy you had telephoned me. (FAB to ETB.)

Congratulations, my dear, on being chosen to represent the National Council of Farmer Cooperatives at the agricultural gathering of leaders in London. Ernest Wilkinson told me about it last night. He said, "Tell Ezra I was to the meeting when he was selected." He said that when it was brought up whom they should send to represent them, immediately your name was brought up. He said the whole group just thrilled at the thought of hoping you could go and represent them. He said the wonderful feelings and admiration they have for you are gratifying. (FAB to ETB.)

SUNDAY, APRIL 7, 1946:
AMSTERDAM, NETHERLANDS

This has been a glorious day of meetings, greetings, and blessings among the faithful Dutch Saints.

The building was filled to overflowing at our Amsterdam chapel. Housing is so short it was impossible to rent a larger hall. We held priesthood meeting, public sessions, and an officers' meeting. There was a sweet soul-satisfying spirit in all the meetings, and most eyes were wet with tears as we enjoyed a rich outpouring of the Spirit in all our meetings.

The Saints, having suffered the ruthless occupation by an enemy power, are still suffering much but are true and faithful. It was so sweet to mingle with them, hear their testimonies, and listen to the fervent singing of the songs of Zion. May the Lord add His blessings. (ETB Journal.)

President Zappey reported that nine members of the mission were lost as a result of the war. Thousands of packages sent by the Church Welfare Committee have been gratefully received by the Saints. With the exception of the occupied countries, the need for continued assistance is probably most critical and urgent in Holland and Norway.

The Church buildings at Rotterdam and The Hague, which were seriously damaged during the war, are now being repaired. (European Mission History.)

Today was the happiest day I have experienced since my devoted husband left for Europe.

All of our family except Flora Beth attended the last session of conference. At the morning meeting Elder Thomas E. McKay read a beautiful letter that was written to him from my husband in Europe.

In the afternoon session of conference a grand letter was read by President Smith from him about his work in Europe and the fine members of our Church there.

The Deseret News took our picture, and it was in the paper yesterday. Also in the paper was a lovely article telling of the wonderful work my husband was doing in Europe. (FAB Journal.)

MONDAY, APRIL 8, 1946:
AMSTERDAM, UTRECHT, AND THE HAGUE, NETHER-
LANDS

The mission home at The Hague was badly damaged by V-bombs, but in addition the building was stripped of all windows, chandeliers, etc., by marauders. Doors were removed and most of the paneling was torn off and apparently used for firewood.

Through the cooperation of the American Embassy, most of the necessary materials needed to repair this build-

Frequently all President Benson had to eat was a modest quantity of K-rations.

ing have been secured. Most of the major repairs will be completed within thirty days permitting occupancy. Meanwhile the chapel in Rotterdam nears completion also. (European Mission History.)

At conference our family was so proud of you when President Smith read your inspiring letter to the conference. It was read at the closing session, and the crowds were enormous — the largest of any meeting I have ever attended.

The conference was all so wonderful but, my, we did miss our dear husband and father. But the Lord shall make it up to us, and He is truly blessing us both and our children in so many, many ways. (FAB to ETB.)

Brother and Sister N. P. Olsen, a lovely Danish couple who just arrived here from Denmark, spent the evening with us. They had met and been with my devoted husband in Denmark a few weeks before. Brother Olsen and his wife came out to Utah to go through the temple. (FAB Journal.)

TUESDAY, APRIL 9, 1946:
THE HAGUE AND UTRECHT, NETHERLANDS

Arrangements were made for storage space at a modern warehouse in Rotterdam in which the welfare supplies, which are now arriving in carlot shipments, can be stored. Distribution will be made to the various branches through the mission office.

In this connection several conferences were held with officials of governmental relief agencies and plans discussed to prevent any possible misuse being made of supplies now being received. We were assured of complete cooperation on their part in assisting with our welfare program. (European Mission History.)

While conditions have greatly improved in Belgium and Holland particularly, the situation continues very critical in the Netherlands. That country was stripped of practically everything movable by the invading hordes. As a result, the country is short of clothing, bedding, farm machinery and equipment, all types of railroad rolling stock, automobiles, trucks, and food supplies.

In our contacts with the Saints and leading governmental officials, we were able to get a fairly accurate appraisal of the situation in the Netherlands. Adding to the seriousness of the problem is the fact that the moral tone of the people is at a low ebb and there is much evidence of pilfering, corruption, and selfishness in connection with the distribution of the products that are available in limited quantities.

Newspaper reports regarding the unsavory operations of the two national relief organizations, which are working at cross-purposes in large measure, are in all the papers. This situation, coupled with the fact that these organizations have received the impression that a large part of our products should be turned over for general distribution, has presented a real problem in the Netherlands. (European Mission History.)

I was in attendance at the home of Patriarch Smith and wife to a lovely turkey dinner. Joseph Fielding Smith and wife drove me there. I sat at the table with Elder Harold B. Lee and Sister Adele C. Howells, president of the general Primary. (FAB Journal.)

WEDNESDAY, APRIL 10, 1946:
LONDON, ENGLAND

Arrived in England and, after two hours clearing customs, etc., we drove to London.

It is good to be back although our rooms were piled high with our office and other supplies, and baskets of mail are awaiting our attention.

Was overjoyed to have six letters from my devoted family, all containing good news, love, and evidence of support and righteous living. Ate meals in the office to save time and, after long letter to my loyal wife, retired at midnight. (ETB Journal.)

Everywhere in Europe today food is the principal topic of discussion. Newspapers carry headlines almost daily. This is particularly true of London.

There seems to be great interest in former President Herbert Hoover's arrival in Europe. It has apparently given the people new hope in knowing as they do his knowledge of and interest in the food problem in Europe and his statesmanlike handling of the problem following World War I. He is certainly faced with an unfavorable situation.

The next three or four months will likely be the most critical in Europe from a food standpoint, assuming of course that we get normal crops this fall — and this is almost too much to hope for in view of the lateness of the season and the shortage of feed, fertilizer, farm equipment, and

84

work stock, to say nothing of the weakened physical condition of the people who are laboring on the farms. Spring has opened up earlier than usual in most European countries, and the moisture conditions are below normal. In the meantime, we find people more hopeful as spring begins to blossom out. All along the way we saw people digging roots in the fields and gathering greens of various kinds to supplement their meager diet. (European Mission History.)

THURSDAY, APRIL 11, 1946:
LONDON, ENGLAND

Had lunch today with President Hugh B. Brown and family who have just been released from the British Mission, effective as soon as Brother Selvoy Boyer and family can arrive to take over the work. (ETB Journal.)

SATURDAY, APRIL 13, 1946:
LONDON, ENGLAND

Office all day dictating and reading mail. Received a lovely box of fruit and nuts from my devoted wife and family and newspapers containing a report on part of the conference.

The April 8th issue had a picture of my wife and five oldest children with Captain Badger, who arrived in Salt Lake from Paris. It was a joy to receive this only five days after it was taken by a *Deseret News* photographer. (ETB Journal.)

SUNDAY, APRIL 14, 1946:
LONDON, ENGLAND

At work in office. Attended sacrament and fast meeting in the London Branch and had supper at the mission home. (ETB Journal.)

Elder John A. Widtsoe called at our home. (FAB Journal.)

Brother Hanley brought us up several nice rosebushes and planted them. The electrician came and fixed my oven to the stove. (FAB to ETB.)

Tomorrow I will pick up the lawnmower and, believe me, the lawn surely needs cutting. We've had to wait so long for it to be sharpened. It will be the first cutting, and we will rake it good as you suggested before cutting. (FAB to ETB.)

Know always that we are praying constantly for you—for your health, strength, success in accomplishing the Lord's work—and praying that the Lord will be your constant companion and that the children and I shall always be a support and help to you forever in accomplishing the things you so much desire to do. (FAB to ETB.)

TUESDAY, APRIL 16, 1946:
LONDON, ENGLAND

Office all day. (ETB Journal.)

Your two letters were so wonderful. I've just been walking on air today since I've received them. I have read and reread them. Just can't get my work done, and I don't seem to care either. (FAB to ETB.)

SATURDAY, APRIL 20, 1946:
LONDON, ENGLAND, AND BASEL, SWITZERLAND

Office and then left for Zurich.

We rode to Basel by fast electric train, and in evening attended conference of the Swiss Mission, where I spoke for twenty minutes. (ETB Journal.)

Tomorrow is Easter, and we shall be thinking of you so much and we shall miss you. (FAB to ETB.)

SUNDAY, APRIL 21, 1946:
BASEL, SWITZERLAND

This has been a memorable day for the Saints of the Swiss Mission. We have held an all-day mission-wide conference and dedicated the lovely new Basel chapel.

Meetings began with an officers' and teachers' meeting and continued, with time off only for food served at the building, until 9:15 P.M. It was a joyous occasion.

The large chapel-recreation hall was filled to overflowing, and the Lord blessed us richly with His Spirit. The music was a credit to the people as was their entire program which compares favorably, as does their leadership, with the better stakes at home.

The dedicatory service had 540 people in attendance — 95 nonmembers. I then gave ten more blessings and left for the mission home with a deep feeling of gratitude for the Lord's sustaining power throughout the day and for the love and devotion of the Saints. (ETB Journal.)

Easter Sunday, and we surely miss our wonderful husband and father.

Reed and Mark are making it a lovely Easter for the four girls — hiding Easter eggs, taking the girls to the capitol to roll their eggs. (FAB Journal.)

MONDAY, APRIL 22, 1946:
BASEL, SWITZERLAND, AND ZURICH, SWITZERLAND

In the evening I visited with Brother Badwagen Piranian, former president of the Palestine-Syrian Mission. I hope to be able to reopen this mission soon, the Lord being willing, and hope to visit the people there in the fall. (ETB Journal.)

WEDNESDAY, APRIL 24, 1946:
LONDON, ENGLAND

Conferences today with officials regarding transportation of missionaries from London to continental posts and movement of relief to European countries now under military control. (ETB Journal.)

The baby is getting along just fine now and growing so fat. She has put on several pounds since she has been sick. I have been feeding her more and seeing she gets a lot more rest.

When we mention your name, she just bubbles all over and is just so thrilled to talk about you and see your picture. She talks so much. She can say sentences now. (FAB to ETB.)

Darling, I sent another box of candy and a box of nuts, fruits, paper pads, pencils, etc.

The Lord is surely constantly with me. He is helping me so much, and, T dear, I certainly feel the power of your prayers to help me. The Lord's guiding Spirit is close to me. (FAB to ETB.)

T, this home is just like four walls since you left. It just isn't home without you. (FAB to ETB.)

SATURDAY, APRIL 27, 1946:
SUNDERLAND, ENGLAND

Left Birmingham and drove to Sunderland.

After a lovely lunch at the home of Brother and Sister William Oates, both of whom were young people in their early teens when I was here on my first mission, we attended the first session of the conference in the old chapel on Tundall Road.

It is a source of joy to come back into a district where one has labored on his first mission as a young man of twenty-two years. Fond memories pass through my mind as I contemplate those sweet and satisfying experiences of twenty-three years ago.

I am grateful that, as I look back on that first mission, I have not one single regret. I thank the Lord for His mercy and for the great strengthening of my testimony which came during that period.

I am sorry to find that some who were faithful twenty-three years ago are inactive now. I called on one of these families on my way home tonight and hope to see others before I leave as time permits. (ETB Journal.)

SUNDAY, APRIL 28, 1946:
SUNDERLAND, ENGLAND

Attended conference of Newcastle District and spoke in all four meetings, three of which were public sessions. There were 147 at the evening meeting.

It has been a joyous day meeting those whom I learned to love and with whom I labored twenty-three years ago on my first mission. My feelings have been so tender today it has been difficult to speak. They have all been most kind, and my heart goes out to them in the pure love of the gospel.

After a good supper at Brother and Sister F. William Oates', I ordained Fredrick William Oates, Jr., a teacher and had a good visit with these good people and President Hugh B. Brown and family. (ETB Journal.)

MONDAY, APRIL 29, 1946:
SUNDERLAND, ENGLAND

Left the Oates at Sunderland and, after visiting the spot near the Sunderland railway station where I was mobbed while holding my last street meeting in England in 1923, drove to Carlisle. (ETB Journal.)

We drove from Sunderland to Carlisle, my first field of labor on my first mission. I spent all the time, when not driving, visiting the Saints I had known years ago. It was a real joy, and I hope I did some good. Some of them aren't as faithful as they once were. The branch was closed during the war because there were no missionaries or priesthood. I'm hoping it will reopen soon. I spent nine happy months here after bidding good-bye to loved ones at home. (ETB to FAB.)

Toward evening we went to nearby Gretna Green, Scotland, and visited the notoriously famous blacksmith shop, scene of thousands of runaway marriages performed during the past 150 years over the blacksmith anvil under the laws of Scotland, which eliminated God and the church from the wedding ceremony and united couples simply by declaration of their desire to wed. Its history was very interesting to hear from the lips of the last "priest" who performed marriages here, the last official ceremony having been performed in 1940. (European Mission History.)

President and Sister Boyer, who will take President and Sister Hugh B. Brown's place, called me up. I am going to see them before they leave for England. I want to give them a box of cookies (homemade) for you. I wish they could take me with them. I do long for you, dearest, but always I know your work with the Lord comes first, and when your work over there is completed and done well, then we can be with each other again. (FAB to ETB.)

TUESDAY, APRIL 30, 1946:
CARLISLE, ENGLAND

Drove from Carlisle to the Tyne Commission Quay between Newcastle and North Shields. (ETB Journal.)

Along the way we viewed the famous Roman wall, stretching most of the distance between the cities of Carlisle and Newcastle, as we rode along the ancient Roman road which in its present repaired state is still a marvel of highway construction. (European Mission History.)

Cleared customs, had car loaded, and got aboard the *SS Jupiter*, a 2,500-ton Norwegian boat, bound for Stavanger, Norway. (ETB Journal.)

WEDNESDAY, MAY 1, 1946:
STAVANGER, NORWAY

We are many miles from land headed northward to Norway.

The sea was a bit rough last night, but is quite smooth today. We aren't seasick yet, and I believe we'll escape. Hope so anyway!

It is a sobering experience to be where you cannot see land in any direction. As one views the vast stretches of swaying water, he feels so small and dependent. Occasionally we see a sea gull even this far out, and we sighted a mine sweeper this morning. They have cleared a strip three miles wide of mines, and the boats are to stay in this lane for safety while the sweeping process is extended to other vast areas. (ETB to FAB.)

President A. Richard Peterson, his wife, and a number of the Saints were on hand to greet us upon our arrival in Stavanger.

Interviews were held with press representatives of the leading newspapers that evening and the following morning. Arrangements for the holding of meetings here, in Bergen, and in Oslo were consummated during the day.

With the arrival of one carload of clothing, one carload of food, and 300 cases of meat from Zion, the Saints of this mission have been adequately supplied with necessary wearing apparel and many items of food which are still critically short. The housing situation is still most unfavorable and may seriously limit the number of missionaries who will be permitted to enter this land.

Conditions generally throughout the mission are very encouraging, and the faith, loyalty, and devotion of the Saints to the Church are greater than ever before. (European Mission History.)

THURSDAY, MAY 2, 1946:
STAVANGER, NORWAY

We held a meeting at which seventy-one members and forty-two friends were in attendance. Brother Gustav Wersland, the branch president, who led the Norwegian underground forces during the war and who exemplifies —

President Benson, Max Zimmer, and Gustav Wersland look over the "graveyard" of German aircraft in Stavanger, Norway.

through his courage, faith, and many miraculous escapes — the spirit and faith of our Norwegian Saints, reported that through the timely assistance of the Church welfare supplies all members in that branch are being adequately clothed and nourished.

To see the large number of members almost completely outfitted in American clothing makes one feel as though he were speaking to an American audience. The gratitude of the Saints is reflected in their increased activity and devotion to the Church. Too much cannot be said for the feeling of brotherhood this has engendered among our people.

During the day the branch president took us sightseeing and showed us some of the destruction and wastefulness of war. Many evidences were seen of the ruthless disregard for life and property by many members of the occupation forces. We saw large graveyards of wrecked German planes and equipment and great storehouses of ammunition and weapons being salvaged for future needs. (European Mission History.)

SATURDAY, MAY 4, 1946:
STAVANGER AND BERGEN, NORWAY

Many highways north are still snowbound, and a number of bridges still unrepaired, so we found it advisable to leave our car in Stavanger and proceed by steamer to Bergen, where we arrived early Saturday morning.

Here the Saints tendered us a hearty reception, and evidence of the invaluable assistance which has come through the welfare program to these good people could be noted on every hand. They look well and strong and are better clothed and fed now than the average. (European Mission History.)

SUNDAY, MAY 5, 1946:
BERGEN, NORWAY

Held three sessions of conference of the Bergen District with about 240 in attendance. The spirit and program were lovely, especially the program by the children of the Sunday School and Primary. It would have been a credit to the people anywhere in the Church. The Saints were most gracious, and the lovely sunny day one to be long remembered. Thanks to the Lord for it all. (ETB Journal.)

I attended the luncheon of the wives of the General Authorities.

I am going to make you some candy and cookies for Brother Boyer to take over to you. I'll have to make the candy tonight. I am going to give them to him in the morning when he is at the Church offices to be set apart for his mission. (FAB to ETB.)

MONDAY, MAY 6, 1946:
BERGEN, STAVANGER, AND OSLO, NORWAY

Left Bergen last night by boat for Stavanger. The trip was pleasant though quite rough as we crossed the widest fjord. From Stavanger, after bidding the Saints a fond adieu, we left by auto enroute to Oslo.

The beauties of the landscape will always be remembered. Roads were narrow and torturous but generally smooth. The scenery was second only to Glacier National Park and is so different that it really has no superior.

As I gazed on the inspiring valley with its green fields and mountains and hills in the distance and the lovely clear river meandering its way to the fjord looking out to the sea, I was led to exclaim, "Behold what God hath wrought!"

This seemed a day of perfect beauty, except for the absence of my devoted wife and family. We stopped at night in a lovely lodge as the only guests in an ideal, quiet spot looking out on the lovely fjord.

God be praised for His goodness in providing such beauty for His unappreciative children. How I pray for the time when the children of men will cease wars, strife, and selfishness and enjoy what the Lord has provided in peacefully living together. (ETB Journal.)

Seeing the millions of large rocks along the way, neatly piled in massive stone fences close together, as far as the eye could see in all directions — rocks removed from the land to permit cultivation — causes one to marvel at the tedious task involved in earning a livelihood from these small plots of land.

The primitive scenery of this land is most delightful to see. We had to skirt around many fjords along the way and were spellbound by the beauty of Kvinnesdal, considered one of the two foremost scenic beauty spots in the nation. We had comfortable accommodations during our overnight stay at a picturesque summer resort on the shores of one of the many majestic fjords. (European Mission History.)

I just came back from buying some groceries at our old shop-

ping place. I ran into Elder Mark Petersen and his wife. They were enjoying themselves together and slowly and casually buying groceries. I thought how lucky and fortunate they were to be able to spend so much time with each other. (FAB to ETB.)

Went to Church offices to say good-bye to Brother and Sister Boyer, who leave for London and who will be taking over the missionary work in that part of Europe.

I couldn't help but shed some tears when I thought of their being able to see my husband before I would. They were tears of love and appreciation for my husband. (FAB Journal.)

TUESDAY, MAY 7, 1946:
OSLO, NORWAY

Many of the welfare supplies received recently in carload lots have already been distributed to our people. The remaining stores of food and clothing were inspected before leaving for Sweden and found to be in excellent condition. Almost without exception the shipments have arrived intact, and their distribution is proceeding in a very orderly manner. Future welfare needs were ascertained and a program outlined for the inauguration of welfare projects within the mission.

A visit was also paid to the American Embassy to solicit their assistance in securing permission from the Norwegian government for our missionaries to continue their work in this nation, permission which had been refused three days ago. We are hopeful that the cooperation assured us will result in the desired permission being granted.

Government officials at present are very unwilling to admit aliens unless it can be shown that such persons are assured of food and housing upon their arrival. In view of the food and housing situation in Norway, it would appear we will not be able to have missionaries go to that country in large numbers until conditions improve. (ETB Journal.)

Local Church leaders transport welfare supplies via handcart in Oslo, Norway.

The mail today brought the sad news of the passing of Sister George F. Richards, a chosen daughter of God, mother of fifteen children (thirteen living) — a queen if ever there was one. May the Lord comfort Brother Richards, president of our Council and a true Latter-day Saint and prophet of God. (ETB Journal.)

Mark took me to the Deseret Theater players' show "Lady." I was wishing I had stayed at home, but my son thought it would do me good to get out.

I am not going out again for a long time. I don't like to leave home even for two or three hours. When my husband comes home from Europe, then I will enjoy going out. (FAB Journal.)

WEDNESDAY, MAY 8, 1946:
OSLO, NORWAY, AND GOTEBORG, SWEDEN

We talked with President Hugh B. Brown from Goteborg. He informed us that the British government has just ruled that aliens coming to England will not be permitted to stay longer than two months. However, he reported that they had extended this ruling to six months in the case of our missionaries. This, of course, will help very little.

We hope to look into this matter further as soon as we return to London. However, in view of the serious food situation in all of Europe and the fact that it is becoming increasingly serious in England, it is quite likely that the British government will discourage foreigners coming to the country for some months to come. The food outlook for 1947 is not encouraging, and Great Britain will likely feel the pinch of food shortages for a considerable period.

In view of this fact, I am wondering if it would not be well to consider sending missionaries intended for Great Britain to Sweden, Denmark, Switzerland, Czechoslovakia, and France, where the policies of the governments are more liberal at present regarding aliens. The opportunity for missionary work is unusually favorable in some of these countries, particularly Sweden. It would be a great blessing if we could have a hundred missionaries here at the earliest possible date to take advantage of the favorable situation which exists. (European Mission History.)

I receive so regularly such inspiring and beautiful and encouraging letters from my husband. (FAB Journal.)

FRIDAY, MAY 10, 1946:
JONKOPING AND OREBRO, SWEDEN

Inspected proposed building sites and drove to Orebro. Held meeting with Saints and public meeting. At least half of the congregation were nonmembers, and several stayed to ask questions and discuss religion. Loaned three copies of the Book of Mormon and passed out several tracts and pamphlets. (ETB Journal.)

President Benson and Eben R. T. Blomquist encounter this roadblock fortification while traveling in Sweden.

Sunday, May 12, 1946:
Stockholm, Sweden

Arrived in Stockholm and began reading mail, which kept me busy until time for meeting. Spoke to Saints for forty minutes. The chapel was filled. Many friends were present. Music and spirit were excellent. (ETB Journal.)

Today is Mother's Day. My dear husband sent me such a beautiful letter.

The baby, myself, and all the rest of the family went to church this morning.

We took several pictures of the family to send to our dear daddy.

Several called to the home to visit with me, both friends and relatives.

Our baby, who is around twenty months old, looked so sweet today. I bought her a sweet new dress and hat of yellow, new sweater, shoes, stockings — and she's such a dear! (FAB Journal.)

The day was beautiful, and the children were all so kind, and tried so hard to take your place and treat me as you would have done if you had been home. There is no one that could take your place, dearest.

It would have been perfect if we could have had the privilege and honor of your being with us, but we realized that it wasn't to be and are so thankful for you and what you have been and are to us and that you are helping thousands of unfortunate people and doing so much for us as a family by living and doing as you are. (FAB to ETB.)

MONDAY, MAY 13, 1946:
STOCKHOLM AND NORRKOPING, SWEDEN

On this visit we have had more time and have attended many meetings in the branches and in the districts and conferred with local leaders. In doing so, we have found many doctrines and practices which have crept in during the war period which must be corrected. We have discussed the details of these problems with the mission presidents and feel certain, with the help of the Lord, it will be possible to make the necessary adjustments.

What we have seen in the last two weeks only emphasizes the inspiration of the First Presidency in warning the priesthood of the Church regarding the dangers of world doctrines and practices creeping into the Church and the importance of keeping our procedures and practices simple and plain as the Lord intended.

Among the practices we have encountered may be mentioned the following:

Weddings: After the civil marriage, another marriage ceremony was held in the chapel patterned after the ceremony of the state church — viz., the chapel was decorated and lighted with candles, bride and groom would walk up the aisle with all their attendants, kneel at the altar, and be blessed and remarried by the presiding officer.

Prayers. Only ordained elders could be used in opening any meeting with prayer.

99

Speakers. Only presiding officers were permitted to speak at Sunday night meetings. LDS servicemen connected with the U.S. legations, who were former missionaries in the respective countries, were not being used in any capacity of Church activity even though they were fully worthy and willing.

Priesthood: Elders have been organized into quorums instead of groups.

Candlelight. Candles were being used at various meetings and social events.

False Doctrine. All nonmembers belonged to the church of the devil and, as his children, would not be saved. This was driving many otherwise sincere investigators away from our meetings.

Title Changes: Branches were being called assemblies instead of branches, and the mission president was called the mission leader. Some of the local leaders had emphasized that the titles were too American and should be changed to conform with national practices.

Meeting Procedures: Congregational singing in many places was completely eliminated, and in other cases choristers or song leaders have been eliminated. In the British Mission it is a universal practice to stand for a minute of silence at the end of the prayer while the organ plays.

The above will be enough to indicate some of the practices which have crept in during the war period. I am sure that all of them can be corrected in the spirit of kindness and love without any serious offense.

The local brethren have done a remarkable work and have given unselfishly of their time and means in the furtherance of the work of the Lord, but thank the Lord the war did not extend for a ten-year period! Otherwise, I fear we would have found crosses and crowns on every pulpit and many of our practices and procedures so far removed from the standard procedures of the Church that it would be difficult to differentiate between our practices and the practices of the world in many matters. (European Mission History.)

At 8:30 this morning the telephone rang and my precious husband was trying to talk to me over the phone from Sweden. The operator said it would take some time to get the call through. She just now called and said the call couldn't get through. When my husband called me a few weeks ago from Basel, Switzerland, he said it usually takes three days before they can get the call through.

I know my husband will keep on trying. He is so thoughtful and good and precious in every way. I think he was trying to get the call through, especially for Mother's Day greetings and love to me. I appreciate his efforts and knowing he tried to call me. (FAB Journal.)

Tuesday, May 14, 1946:
Norrkoping, Jonkoping, and Malmo, Sweden

The prospects for missionary work in this mission were never more favorable. People generally have adopted a very friendly attitude, and goodly numbers of friends and investigators are responding well to the limited missionary activities now carried on.

Our members are very enthusiastic about the possibility of launching a building program throughout the mission, and every effort is being made by them to assist in the establishment of comfortable Church buildings throughout the mission that will be a credit to the Church and to the communities in which they live.

A few days prior to our arrival in Sweden, Elder C. Fritz Johansson, former acting mission president of the Swedish Mission, who had been called during our former visit to labor as a missionary in Finland, left with a companion to begin his labors in that great land. The prospects for a rich harvest in that field appear very opportune. In connection with his missionary activities, a survey will be made of the present and future welfare needs of our members there. Most of these will be supplied by the Swedish Saints in response to a recommendation that they organize such welfare projects as will enable them to care for the Finnish members of this mission.

Conditions generally in Sweden are conducive to large numbers of missionaries from Zion being sent to that land. President Blomquist observed that he believes this nation to be more receptive to the gospel now than ever before. All necessary books, pamphlets, and tracts are being secured in preparation for extensive missionary activities. (European Mission History.)

We are surely kept busy with Relief Society work. We (all the wards) are making hundreds of rag rugs to help with the Church welfare. We have our own loom and are weaving them ourselves, the sisters coming to the ward countless extra days of the week to work so hard on making these rugs. (FAB to ETB.)

THURSDAY, MAY 16, 1946:
COPENHAGEN AND AARHUS, DENMARK

Left Copenhagen by train for Aarhus. Was met at the train by the branch presidency and other brethren, who presented me with a lovely bouquet of flowers.

Spent afternoon visiting and writing to my family and had a good bath—the first since Saturday.

Attended and spoke at meeting tonight. The hall was full to overflowing. (ETB Journal.)

The meeting hall in Aarhus would not accommodate all those present, so the brethren had installed a public address system so the entire proceedings could be broadcast to some fifty people seated on benches provided in the lovely front yard of our chapel there. Many passersby and curious neighbors also listened with interest. (European Mission History.)

I ran into Brother George F. Richards, and he told me how much he appreciated the lovely letter you wrote him.

102

You asked about Sister Richards and her passing. She took pneumonia very suddenly and passed away so quickly. She had attended the April conference, and her husband in his conference address paid her lovely tributes and compliments and said how much she had meant to him, etc. (FAB to ETB.)

FRIDAY, MAY 17, 1946:
AARHUS AND AALBORG, DENMARK

One new branch has been organized since the missionaries were evacuated some six years ago, and another branch will be organized shortly. Throughout the land great interest is being shown by the honest in heart for the gospel message, and the opportunities for missionary work are most favorable. The present national policies are conducive to large numbers working here with the people. (European Mission History.)

During the war years this mission sent considerable relief supplies to Norway and Holland, and the spirit of welfare activity is already deeply rooted here. (European Mission History.)

President George Albert Smith is just fine. I have seen him several times lately, and he is making trips here and there. (FAB to ETB.)

SATURDAY, MAY 18, 1946:
AMSTERDAM, NETHERLANDS

President and Sister Cornelius Zappey were at the airport in Amsterdam to meet us in a new Citroen car which, during our recent visit there, we had arranged for them to purchase for use in this mission. This has greatly facilitated their work inasmuch as all types of transportation in Holland are still badly crippled.

We were pleased to note that the mission home at The Hague, which was quite seriously damaged by a V-2 bomb and resultant pilfering, has been largely restored. Addi-

103

tional materials needed were authorized for purchase. It is impossible to purchase any type of beds at the present time, so temporary beds have been constructed from the lumber in which some of our welfare supplies for the mission have been shipped.

The first carloads of welfare supplies have arrived, but most of them have not yet been unloaded due to strikes at the waterfront. Those unloaded thus far appear to be in good condition. A survey of the needs of all members in the mission has been conducted, and arrangements to quickly distribute the needed articles, insofar as they are available, have been made.

Although this nation has made a remarkable recovery during the past few months, the need for assistance is still quite acute. The Saints are deeply grateful for all the assistance that has been given them.

A farewell testimonial and banquet were given the retiring mission presidency this evening by the Saints of the Rotterdam District. We were pleased to participate and see the splendid feeling of brotherhood that exists among these people. Following the testimonial, a special baptismal service was conducted at which nine new members were added to the Church. (European Mission History.)

Sunday, May 19, 1946:
Amsterdam, Netherlands

This day will be long remembered. We held conference all day with the devoted Saints from all parts of the Netherlands. They turned out in great numbers, and hundreds were unable to gain admittance although we had loud speakers in the basement hall.

The sweet reception, as I walked through two lines of Boy Scouts and was presented with a lovely bouquet and plant in a large wooden shoe as I reached the front of the hall, brought tears to my eyes as the vast audience stood as I entered. I know it was not me but the office I represent that they honored, and how humble it makes me feel as

104

I witness the love and loyalty they show a representative of the General Authorities. How I pray I shall never do anything to weaken their faith and love. (ETB Journal.)

We held our largest conference so far in Europe. President Zappey referred to you and the children in the big conference attended by over 700 people. He read a few lines he had copied from Barbara's letter where she told about missing me, especially Mother, and how you were "pretty sad at times, but we all try to cheer her up the best we can." (ETB to FAB.)

Many stood the entire time during a meeting of over two hours. Some of the Saints had stood for three hours on a bus or train coming to the meeting and then had to stand throughout the entire meeting. Later we asked that all such people be given preference in the next meeting.

They all do whatever they're asked to do in a real spirit of devotion. They truly have the real love of the gospel in their hearts. I am so encouraged over the prospects for work here. I feel sure we'll baptize many hundreds in the next few months.

How we need missionaries! Three have arrived and eleven more are enroute, but we could use two hundred at once! (ETB to FAB.)

These meetings were all that one could ask for with one exception—there was not a hall large enough to hold all the people. Many were turned away, others were seated on the floors, standing in the aisles, and seated in classrooms below the main assembly hall listening to the proceedings over the public address system. It was inspirational to see this great gathering, and their singing was a real credit to any conference.

There is urgent need for a new building to accommodate the members and friends in Rotterdam. We formerly had two branches here, one being destroyed during the blitz on Rotterdam, but now both branches are meeting in one meetinghouse. (European Mission History.)

There is a wonderful spirit in this mission. The field is white already to harvest. Hundreds of new investigators are inquiring about the Church. Many of these are from the upper class in the nation and have no need of or particular interest in any type of material assistance. Every precaution is being taken to insure that all new members are truly converted and not just applying for baptism in the hope that they may become recipients of Church welfare assistance.

Housing facilities for missionaries are very scarce, but every effort is being made to secure quarters so large numbers of missionaries may come to this land. (European Mission History.)

MONDAY, MAY 20, 1946:
LONDON, ENGLAND

At the suggestion of the First Presidency, I previously accepted an appointment to represent the National Council of Farmer Cooperatives on the five-man delegation from the United States to the first International Conference of Agriculture Producers at which thirty-one nations participated. (European Mission History.)

I met with the American delegation to the International Conference of Agricultural Producers in a preliminary meeting at the Dorchester Hotel. (ETB Journal.)

All delegates were presented to the King and Queen and then honored on the eve of the first session at a lavish reception and dinner at the Savoy Hotel as guests of the National Farmers Union of England and Wales. (European Mission History.)

After I had some pleasant talks with various delegates about the Church, we ate a lovely dinner.

It is a fine group of men, but what a contrast in atmosphere in this tobacco-filled room with tables laden with liquor and the atmosphere of our conference in Holland yesterday. (ETB Journal.)

TUESDAY, MAY 21, 1946:
LONDON, ENGLAND

Met with American delegation and joined the first plenary session at Church House along a large U-shaped table running out from the speaker's table with markers indicating each national delegation. It was an impressive sight to see leaders from thirty-one leading agricultural sections assembled.

The language used is English, although the delegations from France, Belgium, and Luxemborg have asked for time after each important statement to allow their translators to give the purport of each.

In the evening a formal reception was held at Lancaster House, St. James. (ETB Journal.)

THURSDAY, MAY 23, 1946:
LONDON, ENGLAND

International conference committee meetings all day.

Tonight President and Sister Selvoy Boyer, new president of the British Mission, and eleven missionaries for Holland and three for Denmark arrived in London. (ETB Journal.)

The leak in the gutter near the front door I will have checked on.

I have had men up several times to fix the stove, toilet, sprinklers, a leak on the front sidewalk.

Brother Hanley insists on putting some more flowers in place of the tulips that you planted and were so lovely that have all

President Benson participates as the U.S. delegate to the International Conference of Agriculture Producers in London.

died down now. He is coming up right soon to put more flowers in for us. (FAB to ETB.)

Thanks so much for the post card you sent me of the two bears hugging each other. I wish it could have been you and me hugging each other, but it won't be long before we can enjoy that with each other again. (FAB to ETB.)

FRIDAY, MAY 24, 1946:
LONDON, ENGLAND

Office and conferences all day. President and Sister Boyer called at the office and brought presents from my ever-loyal wife. (ETB Journal.)

SUNDAY, MAY 26, 1946:
LONDON, ENGLAND

A day to be long remembered because I talked for five minutes to my darling, devoted wife and sweetheart and my sweet family—first Flora, then each child, and then my dear wife again.

How my heart filled with emotion and deep gratitude as I heard their dear voices—those I love even as life itself. I am deeply thankful for the wonders of science that make this glorious experience possible. The Lord be praised for His Spirit which has blessed His children and would do so even more if we'd live worthy of it.

I'm most grateful for my ever-loyal family. No man could ask for sweeter, cleaner children—more devoted to the Church and all that's fine and good. How I thank the Lord for them and especially for my true companion, who is all a man could ask for in a wife and mother. To her goes most of the credit for the excellent training of the children and the little I've been able to accomplish.

Of course, we both give the Lord full credit for all things. She constantly reminds me and the children of this important fact. May the Lord bless and keep her and the children and exalt us in His celestial kingdom as a family unit unbroken.

I attended Sunday School in the London Branch and spoke to the adult members.

I attended a conference of the U.S. delegation to the International Agricultural Conference of Farm Organizations. (ETB Journal.)

We were a very happy family because our wonderful husband and father called from London, England. He talked to his six children too. It was grand to hear his dear, kind voice again.

He wanted to know how we all were, and wanted me to go to the doctor and be checked. I have been needing an operation, but when my husband was called as president of the European Mission, we put off having it.

I have been blessed by the Lord, and as long as we do as we are told by the Church authorities, we have no need to worry. (FAB Journal.)

I sent you a box with dried fruits, nuts, towels, pins, needles and thread, pads, etc., a few weeks ago. Hope you get it okay. By now you should have received the box of gum and hard candy drops. (FAB to ETB.)

MONDAY, MAY 27, 1946:
LONDON, ENGLAND

Attending conference. In the evening I visited the headquarters of the Oxford Group Moral Rearmament and had a pleasant visit with some six of their young leaders.

At the close of the conversation, at their request, I led the group in prayer and received an invitation to return, which I hope to do. This is a constructive force based on some of the basic principles which Christ taught and a recognition of the power and existence of the Spirit of God, which will lead and guide people who place themselves in tune with it.

I hope and pray they may be led to investigate the truth of the restored gospel. To Latter-day Saints, there is nothing new in what they accept. It is but a small part of the glorious plan of salvation vouchsafed to the Latter-day Saints for the blessing of the children of men. (ETB Journal.)

I believe I'm the happiest man in all the world this morning. I've had a most peaceful and restful night's sleep after an experience I shall never forget. It was a joy that defies description to talk to you all on the telephone last night. It was a bit of heaven on earth.

How I thank the Lord for the telephone and the blessings of science which made last night's experience possible. You'll never know how good it was to hear your sweet voice, darling, and the brief but affectionate greetings from the children. (ETB to FAB.)

TUESDAY, MAY 28, 1946:
LONDON, ENGLAND

Committee meetings of international conference. Attended a branch testimonial for President Hugh B. Brown and family. (ETB Journal.)

I am still walking on top of the air, thinking of the joy and satisfaction that I and the children received in talking to you over the telephone from London. It was so good to hear you laugh over the phone, and it was so soul-satisfying to hear your sweet dear voice again.(FAB to ETB.)

President J. Reuben Clark has told others that he feels that it was too much for our ward to expect me to be a counselor in the Relief Society when I already have such a big load to carry with you gone. (FAB to ETB.)

THURSDAY, MAY 30, 1946:
LONDON, ENGLAND

Resumption of plenary sessions of conference and special caucuses to adjust differences. It appears that the Constitution Committee report will be unanimous. Unity is hard to win, but the effort is worth it. (ETB Journal.)

FRIDAY, MAY 31, 1946:
LONDON, ENGLAND

The report of the Constitution Committee, where I've been serving when not in the Cooperative Committee, was unanimously approved in good spirit.

The conference came formally to a close at 6:00 P.M., followed by an hour or so of visiting at a buffet supper. Many fine friendships have been formed which I hope to preserve in the interest of the work of the Lord. (ETB Journal.)

The delegates representing the thirty-one nations all

111

seemed to be men of high moral character who devoted themselves conscientiously to the job at hand. From the very beginning there were differences in both objectives and methods, but there was a spirit of give and take and a frankness of discussion throughout the conference which was most refreshing.

The spirit of this group of farm representatives was the most outstanding single feature of the conference. Most of them had never met before, but as they continued their deliberations through eleven days there developed bonds of friendship and a warmth of spirit that was most heartening.

While the conference closed on a very high note and while much good will no doubt result from this meeting of farm leaders from all parts of the world, yet the most difficult part of the projected program lies ahead. A twelve-month period for the various nations to carefully think through some of the matters discussed and considered in the excitement of the first international conference of farm leaders may tend to temper somewhat the action which most of the countries were ready to take immediately.

The National Farmers Union of England and Wales, which served as host for the conference, did everything within their power to make the visit to England most profitable and pleasant. Many tours, receptions, and social functions were arranged, including a visit to their Majesties, the King and Queen, agricultural shows, experiment stations, farming areas, estates, etc.

In this conference much consideration was given to the food problem. Perhaps the best summary of the world food situation was given at the concluding plenary session by Sir John Boyd Orr, member of Parliament and head of Food and Agriculture Organization, who flew from Washington, D.C., to address the closing session. Sir John, a Scotsman past seventy years of age, is recognized as one of the world's authorities on world food production, demand, and distribution. He had just attended a meeting of FAO

112

and participated in the establishment of an International Emergency Food Council, with representatives of twenty nations in attendance.

The substance of his summary was that with the 1946 harvest, acute shortages of food would continue the 1946-47 crop year. He stated that the only hope for enough cereals to feed the world in 1947 was through emphasis on maximum production of cereals and the diversion of grains used by animals to direct use as food for humans.

In view of the conference proceedings and findings, the vision of the General Authorities of the Church in reemphasizing the great importance of continuing and expanding the Church welfare program stands out in bold relief, and the inspiration behind the Word of Wisdom, given to the world 113 years ago, concerning the Lord's will regarding man's diet, presents a real challenge to all the world.

Throughout the conference many opportunities were afforded to discuss the Church and its program with many of the delegates from several countries, and their response was most gratifying. I was pleased to accept the invitations of many of these men to contact them further when I visit their respective countries. (European Mission History.)

Attended John H. Taylor's funeral. Brother Taylor stayed at our home several nights when we lived in Washington, D.C. He was a grand man and was always so kind and thoughtful of myself and children. (FAB Journal.)

SATURDAY, JUNE 1, 1946:
LONDON, ENGLAND

Saw a matinee of "Song of Norway" showing life and music of Grieg. It was exquisite and most enjoyable. Wished my family could have seen it.

Retired early with a bit of a cold.

Received lovely encouraging letters from my devoted family. (ETB Journal.)

SUNDAY, JUNE 2, 1946:
LONDON, ENGLAND

In room all day with a slight cold and sore throat. Stayed in bed until 1:00 P.M. and doctored myself. Later prepared a bulletin for mission presidents.

Alone all afternoon and evening, but it seemed good. Am feeling much better. (ETB Journal.)

TUESDAY, JUNE 4, 1946:
LONDON, ENGLAND

Office until noon. Then met President Hugh B. Brown and were the guests of Captain Bing, member of Parliament, at lunch at which we discussed the problem of having our missionaries permitted into England. Captain Bing was very much interested and said he'd do all possible to help us. He introduced us to another member of Parliament with whom we discussed the matter.

The captain also took us into the House of Lords Chamber where Commons are now meeting while the House of Commons Chamber, destroyed during war, is being rebuilt. We also saw the House of Lords sitting as a court and saw the speaker march in with his retinue of attendants just before Commons was to meet. (ETB Journal.)

WEDNESDAY, JUNE 5, 1946:
LONDON, ENGLAND

To airport intending to fly to Frankfurt and Berlin. Weather prevented.

Went to House of Commons to introduce President Boyer to Captain Bing. Later was guest of Bing's at debate of foreign situation in House of Commons. Heard excellent analysis by Winston Churchill and Prime Minister Attlee. (ETB Journal.)

FRIDAY, JUNE 7, 1946:
LONDON, ENGLAND

Bade President Hugh B. Brown and family good-bye as they left for Zion via Liverpool. President Brown has

Flora Benson poses with her children—Barbara, Bonnie, Beverly, Flora Beth, Mark, and Reed—in front of their Salt Lake City home.

done a good work in England and the people love him. (ETB Journal.)

Took Barbara, Beverly, Bonnie, and Flora Beth to the Lion House to dinner. I bought four dresses alike for them, and they surely look adorable.

I took the girls in to shake hands with President Clark, Apostle Lee, and others. Everyone admired them, and they are sweet beautiful girls.

The Saints from Sweden sent lovely ribbon for the girls' hair. The color is blue and gold, their country's flag colors.

We all, including mother and the four girls, had our hair in braids and each wore the ribbons on the top of our heads. (FAB Journal.)

SATURDAY, JUNE 8, 1946:
LONDON AND ROCHDALE, ENGLAND

We had a lovely Gold and Green Ball—nine queens and eighteen attendants. They were all lovely Mormon girls. I was proud of them.

115

I longed for you many times, especially during the dance. Of course missionaries don't dance, but how I would have loved to dance with you, darling. (ETB to FAB.)

SUNDAY, JUNE 9, 1946:
ROCHDALE, ENGLAND

Conference meetings all day. The meetings were a joy—full of the spirit of love, unity, and gratitude. The largest session had over 500 present and all were well attended. (ETB Journal.)

At the afternoon session, a large group of LDS Boy Scouts participated in a most impressive presentation of the colors at the beginning of the session. Prior to this presentation, these Boy Scouts and a number of Beehive girls marched around the town hall square to the music of their twenty-piece drum and bugle corps. They are a most enthusiastic and well-disciplined group of whom the Church may be justly proud.

The latter part of this session of conference was devoted to the presentation of a most impressive symbolical pageant depicting the war between good and evil, entitled "Truth Triumphant." (European Mission History.)

Attended June Conference. All of the family attended three meetings today. We enjoyed them very much, and especially hearing a lovely telegram that was sent from my dearly beloved husband, who sent it from Europe. (FAB Journal.)

MONDAY, JUNE 10, 1946:
ROCHDALE AND LONDON, ENGLAND

Before attending a second meeting with branch and district presidents, we visited our Boy Scouts at their camp area. A drenching downpour of rain had forced them to abandon their tents and seek shelter in a nearby farm estate. Though thoroughly soaked, their spirits were high,

116

and they sang enthusiastically after they got started. (European Mission History.)

The expressions of testimony and gratitude manifest in the general priesthood and Relief Society meetings this morning were evidence that the spirit of the conference had been received and that a new era for the gospel in Great Britain had been inaugurated.

This conference has been most successful not only in winning the love and confidence of the people, but in lifting the Saints from their spirit of war depression to new heights of enthusiastic missionary endeavor. A new era of expansion is on the threshold. (European Mission History.)

TUESDAY, JUNE 11, 1946:
LONDON, ENGLAND

The lovely box of dried fruit, nuts, candy, pads, towels, pencils, pins, and thread arrived this morning just in time. I'm taking them to Germany with me for the children. They'll be so grateful. The pins will be useful here as the laundry, when we can get any done, takes off most of the buttons. I haven't had a shirt laundered right since coming here except when Saints have done it.

You almost keep us in food — one more proof I have the most thoughtful wife. Really it's true! (ETB to FAB.)

The Lord just opened the way so I completed a telephone call right through to Berlin, the first into the occupied areas since I've come here. (ETB to FAB.)

FRIDAY, JUNE 14, 1946:
ESBJERG, DENMARK, AND KIEL, GERMANY

Held a meeting with the missionaries, after which administered to some of the Saints.

Left for Kiel, Germany. At border were threatened to be held up, but after some persuasion we were permitted to go through even though we had not received our military orders. (ETB Journal.)

We arrived in bombed-out Kiel to find that the telegram sent the Monday before had not yet arrived notifying the district president of the meeting. The local brethren wanted to borrow bicycles and ride around to the various Saints and out to the little branches some miles away and tell them to come to the meeting that night.

When we told them not to do this, they said, "President Benson, you won't go away until we've had a meeting with you. This is the happiest day of our lives." After some consideration, we promised to return here for a meeting Sunday night although it would be out of our way some 150 miles. (ETB to FAB.)

President George Albert Smith called over the phone and inquired as to how we were getting along. He said that my husband was doing a marvelous and wonderful work in Europe as president of the European Mission. President Smith said, "He is accomplishing things that none of us others could have accomplished. (FAB Journal.)

SATURDAY, JUNE 15, 1946:
KIEL AND BREMEN, GERMANY

After visiting briefly with local and district officers and arranging for a meeting with the Saints, we left for Bremen without military orders.

Near Hamburg, through the courtesy of the British authorities, I was able to call Frankfurt regarding our orders. Received no personal assurance we'd receive them but, feeling sure the Lord would open the way, we drove on and entered the USA conclave and drove into Bremen.

After careful checking, I cabled the First Presidency to route all welfare supplies via Antwerp, Belgium, and Geneva according to first instructions. Also cabled the International Red Cross in Geneva to divide up the two shipments for Munich and Austria so part could go at once to Kiel, Hamburg, the Ruhr, and Frankfurt.

Held a lovely meeting with the Saints and visited with them until 9:00 P.M. (ETB Journal.)

In a meeting held with the Saints in Bremen, 240 were in attendance, the greater part of which were friends and investigators. Here, as in the other cities, we found our members true and faithful, devoted and optimistic even though all of these large cities are seventy to ninety percent destroyed. (European Mission History.)

Brother Toronto, the newly appointed president of the Czecho-slovakia Mission, just called in to see me with his wife and to say good-bye and to be able to tell you he had seen me and that I am feeling fine and send you all my love. (FAB to ETB.)

SUNDAY, JUNE 16, 1946:
HAMBURG AND KIEL, GERMANY

This day will linger in my memory forever.

Left for Hamburg for meeting of priesthood and officers.

We held a general session with the large hall, one of the very few not bombed out, filled to capacity and people standing. Nearly 500 attended.

There were the largest numbers of children I have seen at any meeting in Germany. They very beautifully addressed their greetings to me and presented me with some lovely flowers, and one little girl gave an original poem. I've never seen lovelier children anywhere over here, although they were pale and thin.

Just before the closing song, I had all the children eight and under line up in the middle aisle and, as they walked past me, I gave each one some gum or candy from those you and the children sent. President Zimmer said they'd been sent by my family for the German children. There must have been fifty to seventy-five children. I had to break

119

some of the gum and candy (Life Savers) in two to make it go around.

These sweet, eager but polite little ones almost broke my heart as they looked up with their large eyes and pale faces filled with gratitude. They continued to thank me every chance they got until we drove away.

Then I had all mothers with babies come up, and I distributed a bar of soap (which you sent) to each and a few safety pins, needles, and thread, and an orange which we had coaxed from the army chef in Bremen. Flora dear, you'll never know how much these few little things meant. These women hadn't seen an orange for six-and-one-half years and hadn't had a bar of toilet soap or any pins or needles for years. They couldn't hold back the "ahs" and "ahas" as they saw them and yet they were most polite. You could see they'd starved themselves to try and give more to their children in true mother spirit.

How I wish I could have had baskets full of things — especially food — to give them. If I could have for each of these families the food wasted in the average American home, it would be much more than their total food supply at present. (ETB to FAB.)

There was much feeling of love and gratitude in the meeting. Many tears were shed.

No people could show more love for a church leader than that which these dear people showed me. The spirit of the meeting was excellent, and our hearts were warmed by the Holy Spirit. Somewhere over 400 attended. They stayed in their seats from 8:30 A.M. to 3:00 P.M. Some ate a little black bread or some chicken feed in water for lunch. (ETB Journal.)

I shall ever remember the scene of these sweet, innocent victims of the ravages of war — humble in their gratitude for the gospel, with no trace of enmity or hatred in their hearts. Surely when the Lord chooses the most faith-

120

ful, these, His suffering children, will be among those most blessed. I shed tears with them, gave what encouragement I could, and left my blessing and love with them. (ETB Journal.)

Here's a thrilling story of the spirit behind the Church welfare plan. It has possibly had its parallel in many cities, but this particular instance is worthy of being called to the attention of the Church membership.

Screaming air raid sirens and unusually active anti-aircraft batteries announced the beginning of the thousand-bomber annihilation raids upon Hamburg, Germany. Before the night had passed, the city was a mass of flames and a smoldering wreckage. Among the thousands of casualties resulting from this first concentrated bombing raid were twenty-eight Latter-day Saints listed as dead and a larger number seriously wounded.

During the following two weeks bombers by the hundreds and by the thousands continued to pour their bombs upon this once proud and beautiful city. When the fires finally subsided and the smoke cleared away, Hamburg had been leveled to the ground. Hardly a building was left standing in the entire area. Somewhere in all the debris were thousands upon thousands of dead and many more thousands of wounded either receiving emergency treatment underground or in overcrowded hospitals nearby to which they had been evacuated.

Brother Otto Berndt, the district president of the Hamburg District, although he found himself bombed out for the second time and homeless, called together the members of the Church who could be contacted to determine the losses sustained and the relief and rehabilitation needs of the Saints comprising the five branches in Hamburg.

It was learned that of the 300 members of the St. George Branch more than sixty had been killed and a larger number were receiving medical treatment. The other four branches, though smaller, suffered proportionate losses. Nearly all were homeless and many had lost practically every piece of clothing, all of their provisions, furniture, etc. It was mutually agreed that insofar as possible all should share alike in the things which were yet remaining in the possession of the Saints. Family after family brought their entire stores of clothing, food, and household supplies and shared them with their brethren and sisters who were destitute.

Many items of clothing were impossible to supply from this source, so a relief fund was established to which all contributed, according to their abilities to do so, and these funds were made accessible to the Relief Society for the purchase of materials with which to patch up and remodel old garments as well as to sew new ones. The needs of all were supplied according to their particular requirements, no charge being made to any of them.

Of the five branch meetinghouses in the area, only the Altona Branch chapel remained. This hall was used as a temporary barracks for a large number of homeless families, and the remainder were housed in the homes of members whose property still permitted habitation. Groups of brethren were sent out and made purchases of small plots of land in the suburbs upon which they built hastily constructed homes for the members, using what materials could be salvaged from the blasted ruins.

In a remarkably short time the mammoth job of relief and rehabilitation had been accomplished through the application of basic Church welfare principles with which most of these members were quite unfamiliar, but they had responded unselfishly as true brothers and sisters in the spirit of love and consideration for others, which is, after all, the basis of the Church welfare program.

As we met with these devoted Saints in Hamburg—over 500 of them—we found them more united and stronger in the faith than ever before. Three meetings were held and five full-time missionaries called and set apart, all eager to teach the gospel and bring to men and women the message which, if accepted and lived, is the only answer to the ills of the world and its only promise of peace and happiness.

Many of those in attendance were thin, weak, and hungry — their clothes threadbare and hanging loosely from their starved bodies — but in their eyes shone the light of truth and from their lips came a testimony of faith and devotion that should be a testimony to all the Church. There was no expression of despondency or bitterness, only a feeling of love and gratitude for the gospel of Jesus Christ and for their brethren and sisters in whose lives is reflected the true spirit of Mormonism. (European Mission History.)

As we rode back to Kiel to meet the fine Saints here, we saw people along the road and ditchbanks in the country who had walked for miles on Sunday to try and find a few dandelions or other herbs to take home for food. Some take ordinary grass and weeds and cut them up to mix with a little chicken feed and water, which is their meal. I noticed between meetings some would take out of their pocket a little cup partly filled with chicken feed or cereal and water which they would eat cold. This was their entire lunch.

How I pray our welfare supplies will soon reach them. The first shipments for Germany have just arrived in Geneva, Switzerland. The trains are so slow it may take weeks to go 100 or 200 miles. Then too there is so much stealing by desperate people there is great danger of losing it. Of course we must take the chance and pray to the Lord that these desperately needed supplies reach their destination.

We were told the American army has lost millions of dollars worth of food from stealing on the part of hungry people and some rogues who sell it again in the black markets to get gain. It's a strange situation to see the army wasting food and yet refusing to let hungry people even come near the mess hall to take the garbage that is thrown out. People are wasting in one building and in the next starving.

Sweetheart, I didn't intend to write all this sad picture. I have tried to spare you at home most of the heartrending scenes in Europe today. But somehow I just couldn't hold it this morning. It's terrible to contemplate. I know that the Lord permits the righteous to suffer as He pours out His judgments on the wicked. And I know that even amid the suffering the true Latter-day Saints are sustained by His Spirit. They never complain but suffer in patient, sweet silence knowing as they do that soon it will all be over and, if they are faithful, they shall be exalted on high never more to suffer. Thank the Lord for the testimonies which they have. It is most priceless. What would they do without it? (ETB to FAB.)

Monday, June 17, 1946:
Kiel and Hanover, Germany

Left Kiel for Hanover. Held conferences with British military authorities regarding our people and program. Got quarters (billets) at British officers' camp and mess.

Met with about 200 Saints from the Hanover District in a partially bombed-out schoolhouse. There were no lights and, as it poured with rain outside, it was almost impossible for speakers or singers to read. (ETB Journal.)

The building had seven-eighths of its windows out, and cardboard was nailed up to keep out the rain. The entire roof had been bombed and a temporary roof was installed. The balcony was still out and much of the plaster off the walls. The Saints had brought in flowers and plants, including some large ones, which they placed in either end of the hall to cover the riddled walls.

There was a sweet spirit in the two-and-one-half hour meeting. A lovely little girl presented me with some beautiful red roses following an impressive message of love and welcome to me. A little choir of small girls and a piano trio by three children from the same family were most impressive.

The Saints were most grateful for this, our second visit, to Hanover, and some from Bielefeld particularly, where we have no meeting planned, pleaded with us for a meeting. We'll try and leave Berlin early Friday morning and drive through for a meeting that night. There is nothing I wouldn't do for these poor, suffering Saints. (ETB Journal.)

TUESDAY, JUNE 18, 1946:
HANOVER AND BERLIN, GERMANY

Left Hanover for Berlin. There is no serviceman to make the trip with us as we had desired, so with a new "USA" painted on our car front and rear, we started for the Russian Zone, where such unfavorable reports of bad treatment of civilians had come from.

The trip was made on the autobahn in good condition, except for blown bridges and except for questioning by the Russians as we entered their zone. There were only the usual formalities at the barricades.

On arrival we went to the Economics Building at USA headquarters where arrangements had been made.

We called at the mission office and completed plans for church meetings and conferences. In evening attended a meeting of servicemen and women and a social hour. (ETB Journal.)

We received details concerning the recent missionwide conference held in the city of Leipzig — one of the most amazing chapters yet written in the history of any mission in Europe.

The Russian government permitted extensive advertising — the radio carried announcements three times each day for two weeks in advance, posters were on every billboard in the city and in every streetcar, so by the time the conference began, nearly every person in the entire area knew of it. The amazing attendance of 11,985 persons at the various sessions was the result, and the Sunday evening meeting alone attracted 2,082 persons—by far the greatest attendance ever to be present at a meeting of the Latter-day Saints in Europe.

At a special concert, featuring a missionwide chorus of 250 voices and an orchestra of eighty-five pieces held June 10, 1,021 were in attendance, and at the Gold and Green Ball that evening 1,251 participated. The beautiful congress hall at the Leipzig Zoo, which is being rebuilt, afforded excellent accommodations, and hundreds of people became sincerely interested in the program of the Church.

We feel with all our heart that events such as these testify stronger than words of the faith and devotion of our Saints in these war-devastated areas. Railroad officials scheduled two special trains which went from city to city to pick up our members and take them to this great conference. This has been without a doubt one of the outstanding events ever to take place among the LDS people in this land. The spirit of faith and courage it has engendered will do much to strengthen them during this very critical period which they now face. (European Mission History.)

WEDNESDAY, JUNE 19, 1946:
BERLIN, GERMANY

Began efforts to visit Poland and believe, the Lord being willing, I'11 be able to visit the distressed Saints there.

Met in public meeting with 459 Saints and friends at which I was presented with three bouquets of flowers and, after speaking for an hour, I shook hands with all present as they left the auditorium. It was an inspirational meeting and the Lord richly blessed us.

After the meeting we ate some fruit and bread in our room as time did not permit us to have dinner at the army mess. (ETB Journal.)

THURSDAY, JUNE 20, 1946:
BERLIN, GERMANY

The needs of these Saints are still very great, particularly for fats, cereals, and sole leather. We hope to purchase emergency quantities of these items as soon as we arrive in Basel. Arrangements have been made for shipment through the International Red Cross with an office here in Berlin.

There have been no welfare products arrive as yet from Zion, although a letter from the general Church Welfare Committee was received yesterday notifying them of a shipment of clothing from Los Angeles. It is a miracle how the letter came through in view of the mailing restrictions! All arrangements are made for the handling of the clothing and food supplies when they arrive.

We have been able to purchase two used cars, which will help in the distribution to the various branches. The local International Red Cross office is also getting some used trucks, which they agreed this morning might possibly be available for our use.

In order to avoid interference with our program of food distribution, we now plan to break up the various shipments as they arrive at Geneva and send small quantities to the various districts at more frequent intervals.

We will discuss further details of this plan with the International Red Cross authorities in Geneva later this month and have already reached full agreement with their office here in Berlin. If at all possible, in the future food shipment arrangements should be made to include some soap, shoe leather, and wheat as it comes from the elevator. There is also a great need for recreational equipment, but we will check further into the possibility of making purchases locally from the army or from the Red Cross before requesting any shipments from Zion.

Most of our Church funds are still "blocked" in the East German Mission, but they have all been freed in the

West German Mission. All Church funds have been released in the American sector of the Berlin area. Our funds are in a bank in the British sector where the matter of release is still under consideration. We believe that favorable action will be taken before very long.

The need for Church publications is great. Most of the families do not even have a copy of the Bible or of the Book of Mormon. Present restrictions make it almost impossible to bring in shipments from outside the occupied areas. We are trying to make arrangements for printing of the Book of Mormon, so urgently needed, either in Frankfurt or in Berlin. It is estimated that 2,000 copies of the Book of Mormon could have been sold at the missionwide conference at Leipzig had they been available. Bibles are unavailable. However, through the excellent cooperation of the Religious Affairs Branch of the U.S. Office of Military Government (OMGUS) here in Berlin, we believe this situation will be partially taken care of before too long.

We have conferred with many officials and various heads of departments and branches of the armed services and the military government regarding many problems in addition to those mentioned, such as use of interzone telephone and telegraph communications, priorities for building materials to repair Church buildings, prisoners of war, more liberal mail service, youth activities, and many other matters.

The mission presidency was delighted that we were able to complete arrangements for the installation of a telephone—a convenience they have not enjoyed since the mission home was bombed out early in the war. They were also most happy to learn tonight that arrangements have been largely completed for travel into the Polish area for the purpose of visiting those of our Saints still remaining in those sections of Poland which were formerly Pomerania and Silesia in Germany.

Further checking here confirms the conclusion that all of our shipments for Germany, Austria, and Czechoslo-

128

vakia should be made via Antwerp and Geneva at least for the time being. We are building up experience through Antwerp and Geneva that will be most helpful in the future, and we are most encouraged in our relationship with the International Red Cross. They did a very satisfactory job in handling the shipment into Berlin, which we purchased in Switzerland, and their office here is now able to give very satisfactory service. They have just completed arrangements with the Russians for shipments into the Russian Zone on the same basis as in the other zones. We are all happy over this because the greatest need is in the Russian Zone.

While most of our contact with military authorities to date has been with American officials, we are now beginning similar contacts with British, French, and Russian authorities in their respective zones. The prospect is encouraging, although obviously more difficult than with our own representatives. (European Mission History.)

SATURDAY, JUNE 22, 1946:
BIELEFELD, DUSSELDORF, AND HERNE, GERMANY

After breakfast and a night's rest and bath (first in a week), we drove up the Ruhr, the heart of industrial Germany. After some negotiating with British military authorities, we arranged for billets in some rather bare rooms.

Two hours later we learned that a meeting was scheduled in Dusseldorf in fifteen minutes. We drove to the meeting through the ruins of Essen and Dusseldorf and found some sixty Saints crowded together in a home.

I spoke to them for forty-five minutes, and then we drove rapidly back to Herne for a meeting with the priesthood of the district. We viewed the twisted steel and rubble of the once powerful and extensive Krupp works as we rode. I spoke to the priesthood for half an hour and then retired to our quarters. (ETB Journal.)

129

Sunday, June 23, 1946:
The Ruhr, Germany

This has been a glorious day of meetings with the happy but destitute Saints of the Ruhr District. Three meetings have been held. Some 350 were present in the school auditorium.

In the morning session the children performed, and as a feature we listened to fifteen minutes of the broadcast from Radio Stuttgart of the Tabernacle Choir and organ. It seemed almost as though we were in Salt Lake City. (ETB Journal.)

Through the efforts of one of our splendid servicemen, Captain Fred G. Taylor, Jr., who has general supervision of this radio station, this program was inaugurated some weeks ago. It was a thrill to see the electrifying effect this music had upon the audience. The room was filled with inexpressible joy, and the Spirit of the Lord was richly manifest. (European Mission History.)

Monday, June 24, 1946:
Herne, Frankfurt, and Langen, Germany

Left Herne for Frankfurt, where we arrived having eaten our K-rations in the car.

We began conferences with representatives of International Red Cross and local government officials regarding our refugees at Langen. Later held a meeting with some ninety of them from Poland and eastern Germany. (ETB Journal.)

This evening we witnessed the most heartrending scene thus far in Europe. We met in meeting at Langen (near Frankfurt, Germany) with about 90 of 120 refugee Latter-day Saints who have come into the American Zone from Poland. They have been organized into a branch of the Church in a town where we had no members before.

It was an inspiration to see these poor creatures sit with upturned faces literally drinking in every word we uttered. It was a joy to hear them sing the songs of Zion and to feel of their warmth of spirit and their deep abiding faith in the gospel.

After a meeting of an hour and a half, which was altogether too short for them, we mingled among them and took a picture of the group. During our associations not one word of criticism or bitterness was spoken by any member of the group, although they have lost all of their earthly possessions and some of them their entire family. (European Mission History.)

The saddest moment came later when we drove out to the rough barracks where these people are living. There in the rudest of shelters, without any sanitary facilities whatever, we saw from one to four families living in a single room. The first place we visited had four families living in a single room (twenty-two people), where they slept, ate, and lived. Two-decker bunkbeds had been built along the walls on three sides to accommodate the group for sleeping. A small stove in the middle of the rough board floor provided the only heat for the room and for cooking. Beds were made at night on the floor for the younger members.

The occupants range from babies in arms to one lady past eighty years, and there were several young people in their middle teens. These are all persecuted people from eastern Germany, which is now Poland. They are unwanted in their former homes, and they have come to the American Zone seeking refuge, although technically their coming is illegal since refugees from Poland are supposed to go into the British Zone and those from Czechoslovakia into the American Zone.

We were happy, however, to receive permission yesterday for them to remain inasmuch as they have planted gardens and shown a real desire to help themselves. There

President Benson poses with refugee Saints from Poland in Frankfurt.

was a fine spirit among them. It was a thrill to hear one of the members of this group of twenty-two tell about them all kneeling in prayer night and morning together in their rough quarters. (European Mission History.)

Their spirit is good but their condition desperate. I gave them everything edible we could find in the car and took some of the little children for a short ride in the car.

How I hope and pray we can, in spite of military restrictions, get some lumber or barracks and more food, blankets, and clothing and provide at least one room for each family. Will try and purchase immediately in Basel on Thursday curtain material and wire for dividing the large room into a bit of privacy—also barracks, blankets, and mattresses which can be sent to Langen immediately by my car. (ETB Journal.)

We have now established two refugee camps, one at Langen, near Frankfurt, and the other at Wolfsgruen, south of Berlin. At Langen our members are living under most unfavorable conditions in rude barracks. However, we are providing additional space for them through army barracks purchased from the Swiss government. At Wolfsgruen our members occupy a large castle in cooperation with the Russian military authorities. To both camps we are sending food, both that purchased on the market in Switzerland and that being supplied now through shipments made from the Church welfare stocks.

Facilities at both camps are badly taxed, and our Saints continue to arrive from branches in what was formerly Germany but which is now Poland.

It seems quite certain that German people will not be permitted to remain in the area now covered by Poland. Present Polish regulations provide for the removal of 50,000 Germans monthly. We will likely know more of the details regarding this situation following our visit to Poland later this month.

In the meantime, we have authorized the brethren in Berlin to proceed immediately to negotiate with the Russian military authorities for the rental or purchase of lands formerly used as a military training camp. Much of this land can be used for agricultural purposes, but some of it will have to be cleared first. It is intended that the land be divided up into small farming plots where the people can become largely self-supporting and self-sustaining. We hope to be able to purchase some finished barracks and necessary additional lumber and materials for the construction of new buildings. We also anticipate the purchase of horses, cows, pigs, and chickens and possibly the importation of small gardening tools and implements. We expect, of course, that some supplementing food will be provided through the welfare supplies now at Geneva.

Final approval of the project will not be given until after we have contacted the branches which we are able to reach in the Polish area and have an opportunity to confer personally with the brethren of the acting mission presidency in Berlin.

Eighty members, constituting the balance of the membership from the Danzig District, arrived in Berlin and have been located temporarily at Wobesde by Stolp. A letter came through from the branch president in Breslau a few days ago indicating that the three former branches have joined together in one branch and are holding regular meetings, although their general condition is most desperate. The group has apparently acquired a small piece of land on which they are trying to raise some vegetables during the summer months. This letter confirms other information which has been received to the effect that all of our German Saints now in the Polish area will be required to move west to one of the four zones.

The general policy seems to be that these people should move into the British Zone. However, the Russians have shown no disposition to force them to leave their zone providing they can be properly taken care of. To date we are receiving very satisfactory cooperation from the Russian authorities. (European Mission History.)

WEDNESDAY, JUNE 26, 1946:
FRANKFURT, GERMANY, AND BASEL, SWITZERLAND

Left Frankfurt by auto and drove to Basel, stopping at Mannheim to inspect building lots.

Detained at Swiss border for some time and finally had to leave Brother Babbel for a period because of lack of proper visa. Later we cleared the matter and he came to Basel by streetcar. (ETB Journal.)

Attended a summer garden party and dinner given by the General Authorities of the Church. It was held at the home of Apostle Stephen L Richards.

Reed went with me as my partner. Apostle and Sister Mark Petersen called and took us in their new car.

134

We had a lovely time, but I missed having my wonderful husband with me.

The Lord is blessing us both during our separation from each other. But we know the Lord's work comes first. Whatever the General Authorities say, we are to do—we shall know it to be for the best, and we shall always do as they advise and counsel. (FAB Journal.)

THURSDAY, JUNE 27, 1946:
BASEL, SWITZERLAND

We arrived at Basel, where I had a long conference with Presidents Taggart and Zimmer regarding certain matters concerning use of mission home and future work and relationships. Retired at 1:00 A.M. (ETB Journal.)

I was invited to a lovely luncheon party at the home of President J. Reuben Clark. It was a lovely affair. President Clark is most thoughtful and kind to me. (FAB Journal.)

FRIDAY, JUNE 28, 1946:
GENEVA AND ZURICH, SWITZERLAND

The situation with reference to relief needs and distribution regulations is changing daily. For this reason it seems important that every precaution be taken to avoid concentration of large quantities of food or clothing at any one point in the occupied areas. The policy with reference to displaced persons and refugees has not been finally determined.

A number of our people from the area formerly included in eastern Germany, but now in Poland, have already moved into the western zones. To date we have been quite successful, after conferences with the authorities, to get permission for them to remain in areas where we are best able to give them the help which they need. We feel very strongly the importance of maintaining at all times a stock of supplies at Geneva for distribution in accordance with existing policies and the needs of our people.

135

The International Red Cross has now completed arrangements for distribution of foods within the whole of the Russian Zone. We are most grateful for this development. With this and other facts in mind, we have today sent official instructions to them at Geneva for distribution of the food and clothing already received in Geneva. This distribution has been made on the basis of size of districts and need of the people and will provide a small shipment to each of the districts in the East and West German missions and the Austrian District of the Swiss-Austrian Mission.

We are most grateful that the first shipments have arrived and that others are enroute. We are also pleased to note the inclusion of a sizeable proportion of whole-wheat cereals and dried beans and some soap. May I suggest that in future shipments you increase relatively the quantity of whole-wheat cereals and dried beans and peas and reduce somewhat the proportion of canned fruits and vegetables. The inclusion of meat products is greatly appreciated, although if we could have quantities of concentrated fats included in each shipment, it would be even more valuable.

Correspondence with the Saints in the Palestine-Syrian Mission indicates that our members will likely have to leave their present homes for Armenia this fall. The question of transportation of these unfortunate souls, who now become a part of the ever-increasing "displaced persons" group, will likely be an important problem. (European Mission History.)

SUNDAY, JUNE 30, 1946:
PRAGUE, CZECHOSLOVAKIA

Held a meeting with the Saints of Prague in the little meeting hall at the home and mission office where President Roubicek has lived and had his office during the war. There were twenty-eight present.

We had a glorious time, and the Lord richly blessed us. Tears of joy were shed by practically all present. This is the first meeting of the Saints since President Toronto and the two missionaries have arrived, and second only to the meeting I held with them in March, the first since the war.

In the afternoon, with several members of the branch, we rode for an hour and a quarter on the train and walked a mile up a hill to the Karlstyn Hills near the famous castle by that name. Here we stood on sacred ground, at the top of a hill overlooking the castle and valley, where the nation was dedicated to the preaching of the gospel seventeen years ago (July 24, 1929) by John A. Widtsoe. We held a short service during which we sang "We Thank Thee, O God, for a Prophet" and "Count Your Blessings." President Walter F. Toronto told of the opening of the mission and the acting mission president, who had been released at the morning service after six years of service, told of the securing of the plot of ground and the erection of the lovely little monument commemorating the beginning of the work here. I then dedicated the monument. (ETB Journal.)

The site and monument are recognized by the government as a historic landmark, standing as a tribute to the devotion of the Saints even during the most adverse circumstances of the war years. The Saints stood with tear-filled eyes as they heard the prayer of dedication offered upon this lovely spot. (European Mission History.)

MONDAY, JULY 1, 1946:
PRAGUE AND BRNO, CZECHOSLOVAKIA

This is the birthday of my faithful and ever-devoted wife, Flora, whom I love more dearly as the years pass. Arose at 5:00 A.M. and wrote her a letter.

After a breakfast of bread and cocoa, we left by train for Brno. We were met by Saints who greeted us warmly and presented us with flowers.

We went to the home of the branch president, Otokar Vojkuvka, where we had a lovely dinner. (ETB Journal.)

Today is my birthday. I am forty-five years young. The children were very sweet, thoughtful, and kind to me.

I received a beautiful letter from my adorable husband for my birthday. He told me of his deep love for me and how he thanked the Lord for me. All of his letters seem like Mother's Day letters because all of his letters are so full of love and appreciation for me, our religion, and our children. (FAB Journal.)

THURSDAY, JULY 4, 1946:
PARIS, FRANCE, AND LONDON, ENGLAND

Morning spent in conference with President and Sister Barker. Left for London on a rough partially reconverted army plane.

Arrived at my London office to find my desk piled high with mail and several emergency problems awaiting my attention. Spent four and one-half hours opening and classifying mail and talking with officials of the International Red Cross at Geneva.

Was happy to receive letter and several packages from my ever-devoted wife and children. (ETB Journal.)

This is a day of celebration in the good old USA, a land choice above all other lands. Our independence has been somewhat of an inspiration to many other peace- and liberty-loving peoples in various parts of the world. (ETB to FAB.)

President Selvoy J. Boyer of the British Mission reports that the British government has now given permission for visas to be granted to our missionaries called to this mission and has expressed its willingness that the Church resume its full-scale, pre-war activities. (European Mission History.)

FRIDAY, JULY 5, 1946:
LONDON, ENGLAND

At office dictating letters all day and evening. (ETB Journal.)

Clyde Cummings gave me a box of his candy from his store to send to my husband. I enjoy sending my devoted and kind husband boxes of candy, cookies, cake, dried fruits, nuts, and some canned food. He is so appreciative of what the children and I do for him. (FAB Journal.)

SATURDAY, JULY 6, 1946:
LONDON, ENGLAND

Office all day. In late evening, after a most heavy day, saw the picture *Caesar and Cleopatra* in technicolor, now running at the same showhouse for over two years. (ETB Journal.)

I sent a large box of old-fashioned peppermint candy. I thought perhaps you might like to give them to the children, and I also remember you like them real well.

I sent a box of tuna fish, dried fruits, nuts, gum, and bouillon cubes. The bouillon cubes make a nice beef broth. Drop one in a cup of hot water, and it's delicious! Some of the less fortunate Saints may enjoy these, and you would like them too yourself. One little cube could be given to several of the German women perhaps, and it would give them a little taste of something nourishing. (FAB to ETB.)

We are really getting real hot weather, and it certainly keeps me stepping with our fine boys having to leave so early for their work and working so hard.

I too am working hard during the summer, but the Lord is blessing me—although I feel pretty "dozy" at times and "drag" myself around, but still I'll have a lot of pep left for you when you get home. I can still hold my own with any of them. (FAB to ETB.)

MONDAY, JULY 8, 1946:
LONDON, ENGLAND

We continue to receive a large number of letters from members of the Church in Zion regarding their relatives in the occupied areas, requesting that we get relief to them. We are trying to do all we can in this regard; however, in the American Zone particularly relief may be sent direct to relatives of members of the Church through the shipment of parcel post packages or the CARE thirty-pound food packages. The American military authorities seem to prefer the regular eleven-pound parcel post packages. (European Mission History.)

Everyone has been so unusually quick and thoughtful to really put themselves out to do for me since you have been gone. (FAB to ETB.)

TUESDAY, JULY 9, 1946:
LONDON, ENGLAND, AND AMSTERDAM, NETHER-LANDS

Left London for Amsterdam. Met by President Cornelius Zappey at about noon.

Drove to mission headquarters at The Hague, where we had lunch. We then inspected the 15,000 boxes of welfare supplies in the rented warehouse where some fifteen sisters and eight men were stacking, sorting, and taking inventory.

After some pictures, we went to the city planning office and then inspected and selected a lot on which to build a new chapel.

After dinner, telephone calls, etc., at mission home, we drove to Amsterdam, where we attended an opera in the branch. It was a three-hour-long comic opera entitled "Escape."

After some administrations and interviews with missionaries, I retired at 12:30 A.M. (ETB Journal.)

I opened that choice box of candy. We all sang your praises. The cake, cookies, dried fruit, and nuts have kept us living high. It is all deeply appreciated, honey. (ETB to FAB.)

WEDNESDAY, JULY 10, 1946:
AMSTERDAM AND GRONINGEN, NETHERLANDS

Arose early and drove to Groningen across the twenty-mile dike. Here I inspected proposed building sites, held a meeting with the missionaries, and in the evening met with 250 members and a few friends.

The meeting was not publicly advertised because of the lack of space. We hope we can build a large commodious chapel here in this branch of 350. Many will yet accept the truth here. (ETB Journal.)

Deseret News came up and took several pictures of us with some of the things on that the Saints sent us from Europe.

We will send pictures to the Saints in Europe of our family. (FAB Journal.)

FRIDAY, JULY 12, 1946:
STOCKHOLM, SWEDEN, AND ABO, FINLAND

Interview with other reporters and then inspected several proposed buildings as mission homes. None of them were suitable. Conferred regarding mission matters and left by boat for Abo, Finland.

It is a beautiful sunny pleasant day. The water is calm. We rode through the delightful fjords for three hours with wooded land and islands on either side. Boats of various kinds plied the placid waters. Summer homes were in evidence on the shores and lovely sailboats, launches, and motorboats as well as larger craft were everywhere. As we retired at 10:30 P.M., we were well out in the Baltic Seas and, while the waves were a little greater, it was all most peaceful and restful. (ETB Journal.)

SATURDAY, JULY 13, 1946:
JAKOBSTAD, FINLAND

Before docking we were met by a news reporter aboard the ship and were greeted by others waiting at the docks.

The reception was most friendly and cooperative, not only on the part of the people, but by the press and leading civic and governmental groups. They have a very high regard for the American people and expressed their desire to have the Church establish a mission in that land.

Their testimonies were inspiring, and the appreciation expressed for the assistance rendered them through the welfare packages was most sincere. A good many members of the branch were outfitted in welfare clothes and are better dressed than the average people of the community. Many of the welfare products are still kept in the basements for special occasions. (European Mission History.)

The population of three-and-one-half million includes about 300,000 Swedes, located largely on the west and southwest coast. About ten percent of the population is in Helsinki (Finnish) or Helsingfors (Swedish).

Russia has taken over three parcels of land on the eastern border and leased for an extended period a part section in the south. The Finns in the Russian-occupied areas (500,000 of them) are being forced to leave. This presents serious problems of adjustment as the area taken is Finland's richest dairy and industrial area. Russia also moved factories, rolling stock, etc., to Russia as in Germany. The part of Finland occupied by Russia was inhabited only by Finns.

The Germans entered Finland the summer of 1941 and left September 1944. The Finns first accepted the Germans as their protection against the Russians with whom they had war in 1939. Their own safety influenced them. Later, through Allied pressure, they fought the Germans and drove the last of them out into Norway January 1945.

Finland is now paying heavy reparations to Russia, and Finnish taxes are very high. The Lutheran Church is the state church. There are some Greek Catholics.

A recent survey showed that ninety percent of Finns

would like to leave Finland—sixty percent prefered Sweden and thirty percent USA.

The Finnish are fine people. Practically none of them speak both Finnish and Swedish. The Finns need a mission of their own with a president, possibly at Helsinki, from the USA. Their love for Americans is great. We have a brother in Helsinki who speaks English, Finnish, and Russian who could help.

We left Abo and rode on a day coach of ancient vintage. After an hour's wait, we transferred to a pullman with proper sheets. For dinner we had a raw vegetable much like a turnip and one slice of black bread with a little artificial cheese on it, but even so it tasted very good as I was hungry. (ETB Journal.)

Mrs. Hugh B. Brown and daughter dropped in a minute. They just returned from England.

My darling husband had given her gifts to deliver to us. They were most thoughtful and lovely gifts and presents. (FAB Journal.)

SUNDAY, JULY 14, 1946:
JAKOBSTAD AND LARSMO, FINLAND

Arrived at Jakobstad and went to the hotel. Had breakfast of bread and jam and drove out to Grev School in Larsmo for a meeting with the Saints in a schoolroom. As we drove up at the gate of this rural school, I was impressed to see a large U.S. flag flying from an improvised pole so that the tip of the flag hung over the middle of the entrance to the path leading to the schoolhouse. The path was lined with little boys and girls with U.S., Swedish, and Finnish flags. As I walked through the lines, the first children I passed followed me and, in turn, all followed into the schoolhouse with their parents joining at the door.

There were many tears of joy shed, especially when the children sang in English "America" and presented me with a little silk Finnish flag on a metal pole in an inscribed

143

base. Expressions of gratitude for welfare packages were most touching, and frequent reference was made to the fact this is a historic day — the first visit of one of the General Authorities. How they love us!

Forty-two attended the two-hour meeting, after which we visited, took pictures, and then went to some of their nearby small farms for lunch.

We held a public meeting — ninety-one present. After an hour and forty minutes, we closed the meeting and walked off the stand, but none of the congregation would leave. They all remained seated. So we spoke to them more, sang songs, and I even sang as a solo "I Know That My Redeemer Lives."

Over half the audience were nonmembers. It was a most friendly and appreciative group. The schoolmaster, who with his family occupies a small apartment in the school building, expressed on behalf of the group their gratitude to USA for all their help. They were delighted when I told them I'd convey their expressions to President Truman, whom I know.

Returned to hotel at 5:45 P.M. Spent evening reading *Era* and prayers and meditation regarding the Finnish people. (ETB Journal.)

Groceries are surely climbing sky high. Butter is now eighty cents a pound. Milk has gone up, bread, meat, and so many things are higher. (FAB to ETB.)

TUESDAY, JULY 16, 1946:
JAKOBSTAD AND LARSMO, FINLAND

We are still in the midnight sun period here. Last night in my room I wrote at 10:45 P.M. without any artificial light. In fact the sun didn't set until after 9:00 P.M. This morning at 3:00 A.M. I awakened and it was broad daylight.

I arose at 4:45 A.M. to keep an appointment with a taxi. We left for Grev School in Larsmo. Here we met fourteen of the faithful Saints and walked one mile to a spot selected last night as the highest elevation in the area and an appropriate place to dedicate this land of Finland for the preaching of the restored gospel.

We formed in a half-moon on the large flat rock from which we could see in all directions for long distances as in the quiet of early morning the glory of God's sunlight shown through the trees. According to previous arrangement, President Eben R. T. Blomquist conducted the little service consisting of the opening and closing prayers, the skillful singing of "Praise to the Man," "The Spirit of God," and "We Thank Thee, O God, for a Prophet," brief historical remarks by President Blomquist, and the dedicatory prayer by me.

The Lord was with us. During the prayer we were overjoyed in our humility to feel powerfully the Spirit of the Lord as we were all moved to tears. Several sobbed like children with gratitude for this occasion and the rich blessings of the Lord which are ours.

Even after the impressive service was over, several of those present bore their testimonies of how the Lord had revealed unto them the happenings of this day. We all seemed reluctant to leave, but after one and one-quarter hours, we quietly left as I led them through the trees and underbrush onto a country road and on to the humble, sweet home of the branch president, where we ate breakfast and visited for an extended period before we left for the city of Jakobstad.

In the evening we held a public meeting in a public hall, the Svenska Garden. About 100 were present and were most attentive as I spoke for an hour and ten minutes with perfect freedom—thanks to the Lord's sustaining power.

The devoted Saints, who were almost all present, were reluctant to leave us. We all sang "God Be with You Till We Meet Again," and after several goodbyes and expressions of love and gratitude, we parted.

As I waved a final good-bye as they went out of sight,

145

I thought silently, "These are the kind of Saints I should like to associate with in eternity! Thank the Lord for the precious experiences of the past three days here and for His kind sustaining power. (ETB Journal.)

WEDNESDAY, JULY 17, 1946:
JAKOBSTAD AND HELSINKI, FINLAND

Arose at 3:45 A.M. to catch a 4:40 A.M. train for Helsinki. To our surprise, when we reached the station, the faithful Saints from the branch were there to bid us a fond adieu. More tears were shed as we shook their hands warmly and then sang "God Be with You" as our train pulled out. As far as the eye could reach, they waved good-bye to us as our train, old and dilapidated, rolled away into the white birch forest.

We rode all day, arriving in Helsinki. It was a long hot ride with practically no food, much dirt, crying babies, and overcrowded cars filled with poorly clothed but good people. We had several fine gospel conversations enroute.

We went immediately to the hotel, where representatives met with President Blomquist and me in my room for over an hour. They were most friendly and interested in the Church and its program. I gave them photos at their request.

We then rushed to our meeting and were pleased to find 250 people present. (ETB Journal.)

This summer is really the most rushing and busiest I have ever experienced, but I am pulling through with flying colors and I am so thrilled and happy for what the future may bring us.

So please excuse me if I neglect in not writing my letters so perfectly because you'll know I am trying to do so many things for us all. I love to write to you so much. It's my chance of entertainment and relaxation and my means of companionship.

I hear of families taking lovely vacation trips. Do you think a thing like that was ever meant for us or will come to us? Perhaps it will come in the next life, or perhaps we wouldn't be happy if we weren't always working the hardest possible. At the same time I do believe the Lord expects us to take care of ourselves and not overdo too much. That's one thing I still will have to learn. (FAB to ETB.)

THURSDAY, JULY 18, 1946:
HELSINKI AND ABO, FINLAND

Held conferences with American ambassador to Finland, also First Secretary and Consular and Third Secretary and Vice-Consular—all of the embassy.

Later called on Mr. M. Asko Ivalo, Foreign Minister of Finland, who assured us every cooperation if we decide to open a mission in Finland.

Left by train for Abo on Finland's best train. We were required to go two hours out of our way because of the area on the south coast appropriated by Russia.

Arrived in Abo and attended our public meeting. There were 117 present—all friendly and seemed appreciative.

After the meeting I visited with a lady who seems quite prominent in Finland. She has a large farming area with her husband, who is a newspaperman, and has a home in Abo and Stockholm and property in Helsinki. She and several others urged us to come to Finland with a mission. They said that the time was now opportune since the Finnish people are more religiously inclined now than ever before and church attendance is at an all-time peak. America is most popular here, and thousands will attend our meetings if given an opportunity. (ETB Journal.)

Spent time contacting leading civic and governmental officials, both American and Finnish, all of whom were most considerate and solicitous of our welfare. Each expressed his willingness to assist wholeheartedly in any missionary activities which we may wish to undertake as a Church. At the urgent request of some of the Finnish leaders, I wrote a letter to President Harry S Truman as follows:

Dear Mr. President: Since early February I have been representing my Church on a religious and relief mission in the various countries of Europe. I have just returned from my first visit to Finland, where I held a number of well-attended public meetings in the principal cities. Everywhere I was received with the utmost kindness. Never at any time or in any other places have I heard so much favorable comment regarding the United States.

At the urgent request of some of the Finnish leaders, I promised to write you and express to you on behalf of the Finnish people their deep gratitude to the American people and their leaders for the unselfish assistance which the nation has rendered to the Finnish people through the years. I am free to admit that these sober-minded, solid, splendid people completely won my heart.

I have noted during my absence from my home in the States the many perplexing problems which confront you. May a kind Providence endow you with wisdom and inspiration in carrying the great responsibilities of your all-important office. Faithfully yours, Ezra Taft Benson. (European Mission History.)

The Finnish people have suffered much through the war. They are humbled, and their hearts are full of anxiety. They are seeking after religion. Attendance in the established churches of that land is greater than ever before.

Now that this land has been dedicated to the preaching of the gospel, we are most hopeful that ways and means to provide them with that opportunity may soon be realized, that the honest in heart of this great nation may enjoy with the Saints throughout the world the sweet fruits of the gospel of Jesus Christ.

The Finnish people were most friendly, have a very high regard for the American people, and showed every indication of wanting us to come into that land and establish a mission. I have never met a more favorable press or a more friendly and cooperative people.

While there are no occupation forces, the Russians control the only important airport some forty-two miles from Helsinki and the chief port, which necessitates the Helsinki-Abo train making a two-hour detour to avoid passing through this now Russian territory. Although the Russians have taken the rich nickel mines in the western part of Finland and much of their rich agricultural lands, the people are not discouraged. Their hearts are full of hope and they are grasping for something hopeful to sustain them. The gospel will fill this need in large measure. (European Mission History.)

Our visit was a joy from beginning to end in spite of the difficulties in communications and transportation, acute shortages of food (even salt is rigidly rationed), and the apparent anxiety of the people over the future. While we have two missionaries laboring now among the Swedish-speaking people and there has been work done sporadically in years past among this group of people, I feel to recommend that serious consideration be given to the early establishment of a mission, to be known as the Finnish Mission, with headquarters in Helsinki. Educators, the press and government officials, as well as a number of the many people who attended our public meetings, gave us every encouragement to establish our work among the Finnish-speaking people.

We were informed that the Finnish language belongs to the Hungarian group and that experience has demonstrated that Swedish-speaking people seem to learn that language most readily. The Finnish people, who were once a part of the Swedish nation, are very friendly toward Sweden. President Blomquist plans to send four to six more missionaries into the Swedish-speaking area. (European Mission History.)

149

SATURDAY, JULY 20, 1946:
STOCKHOLM, SWEDEN

During last night, about midway in the Baltic, we ran into heavy fog which slowed us up considerably — in fact, stopping us completely a time or two.

We arrived four-and-one-half hours late, and were warmly greeted by missionaries and Saints, some of whom were there at the wharf since early morning. The morning dawned lovely and calm, and it was greatly enjoyed as I sat on deck in the sun and finished a letter to my sweetheart.

Held a meeting with the missionaries and a public meeting attended by 245. (ETB Journal.)

SUNDAY, JULY 21, 1946:
STOCKHOLM, SWEDEN

This has been a heavy but happy day of meetings, visits with Saints, and administrations.

Held and spoke at meetings of joint officers, Relief Society and priesthood, branch presidencies, members of mission, and public session. All the meetings were full of spirit and quality. There were 265 at the meeting tonight.

The meeting with members was a testimony meeting and lasted three full hours — and then more wanted to bear testimonies. The first person on her feet was the oldest member, ninety years. President Blomquist says this evening's meeting is the largest gathering of Saints ever held in Sweden.

The Saints were most gracious and kind to me and sang as the last song, in English, "God Be with You." Many tears were shed.

I then performed five more administrations, conferred regarding buildings, ate some lovely strawberries, and retired — grateful for the Lord's rich blessings.

Have received a wire that the new mission president for Denmark, Alma L. Petersen, has just arrived in Copenhagen. Complying with his request that I stop off en-route to London, I have been able to change my ticket even though they reported in Stockholm full bookings from Copenhagen to London for two weeks. Once again the Lord has opened the way. (ETB Journal.)

MONDAY, JULY 22, 1946:
COPENHAGEN, DENMARK

Conferences with President Alma L. Petersen, recently appointed president of the Danish Mission, and Elder Orson B. West, who has been acting mission president since the outbreak of war in 1939. Although the Copenhagen Saints had filled their hall to capacity Sunday to greet their new mission president, they met again on Monday night in even larger numbers. At that time Elder Orson B. West was honorably released and President Alma L. Petersen wholeheartedly sustained in his new assignment. (European Mission History.)

I spoke for three-quarters of an hour, and the music and spirit were lovely. After visiting with the Saints, who gave me a most warm reception, and administering to some, I retired with President Petersen — and after talking problems for another time, slept between 1:00 and 5:00 A.M. (ETB Journal.)

TUESDAY, JULY 23, 1946:
LONDON, ENGLAND

Was made very happy to receive 8x10 pictures of my lovely wife and family. (ETB Journal.)

THURSDAY, JULY 25, 1946:
LONDON, ENGLAND

All day in office dictating and reading letters.
Visas for Poland being delayed. I called Berlin, where I hope we'll find everything all right. We expect to leave here for Frankfurt and Berlin in the morning. (ETB Journal.)

FRIDAY, JULY 26, 1946:
LONDON, ENGLAND, AND BERLIN, GERMANY

Left London for Berlin. We rode in an army transport sitting on hard metal seats. Before we took off, in a cabin that was roasting hot, we received instructions on how to put on the Mae West life preservers and parachutes. The ride was terribly noisy, and the cabin filled with smoke as there was nothing but the metal framework of the plane and no ventilation as in the modern passenger planes.

We arrived in Berlin in the once great German airport and terminal building.

Through some misunderstanding in time, we were not met and so took the OMGUS bus to American headquarters, where Brother Francis Gasser picked us up and took us out to the beautiful home of Brother and Sister Eugene Merrill, formerly of Washington, D.C. He is a son of Joseph F. Merrill and head of the Communications Branch of U.S. Military Government here. They occupy a mansion, the home of Germany's former chocolate magnate.

After a walk through the beautiful grounds, following a chicken dinner, I retired to a bed fit for the kings — or even an average U.S. civilian in military government work. (ETB Journal.)

PART 2:
NEWS OF SUCCESSOR
AND CONCLUSION OF MISSION

Saturday, July 27, 1946: The appointment of Elder Alma Sonne, Assistant to the Council of the Twelve, to preside over the European Mission to succeed Elder Ezra Taft Benson, was announced today by the First Presidency.

Elder Sonne will be accompanied by Mrs. Sonne. They will leave for the mission headquarters in London as soon as arrangements can be made. (Church News.)

SATURDAY, JULY 27, 1946:
BERLIN, GERMANY

Spent day in conferences with military government and mission authorities and in arranging for visit to Poland. (ETB Journal.)

SUNDAY, JULY 28, 1946:
BERLIN, GERMANY

Held meeting with mission presidency and then met with Saints (322) of the Berlin area in a special meeting in the auditorium of a school building. As I entered the hall, little children were standing on benches along the aisle by the wall and, as I walked along, they each threw flowers in my pathway. It was so touching I could not hold back the tears.

We held an excellent meeting, and afterward the people

153

lined the aisle, hallway, and stairs (three flights) and shook hands with me as I made my way to the car.

I was surprised to find the little children, three lines deep, on tables in the hall, where I shook hands with them as they all shouted three times in English, "Good-bye, President Benson."

We held a sacrament meeting with servicemen and U.S. government people and then enjoyed music and good food at Brother Merrill's lovely home, where we closed the day in prayer together. (ETB Journal.)

MONDAY, JULY 29, 1946:
BERLIN, GERMANY

Conferences today with Religious Affairs Secretary, military government, and United Nations Relief Agency (UNRA) officials with whom I was a luncheon guest.

Met the Polish ambassador and received passport visas. Further conferences and arrangement for supplies to take to Polish Saints. These were packed in several cases in the evening in readiness for our journey. (ETB Journal.)

TUESDAY, JULY 30, 1946:
WARSAW, POLAND

Arose and left for the airport. After some weather delay, left and had a most rough ride in an old army transport freight plane — only room for eight passengers (rest of space taken by freight for embassy). On arrival, our plane could not land because workmen, trucks, and cows were on the runway. There is no radio contact with the ground, so we flew low over the field to let everyone know we wanted to land. Then we rode out five miles and turned around and landed on a rough field.

We were met by several guards with machine guns. Had some little difficulty clearing customs and passport control because of difficulty with English and Polish and reluctance of Poles to speak German.

With help of embassy, we were given cots in a room

with five of us together at the Polonia Hotel, the only one intact in the city. Our room was also a sort of club room or meeting place for U.S. news correspondents, so things were lively.

Had a very satisfactory conference with the ambassador and for an hour discussed religious and economic problems.

Later I walked for several miles through this once proud city which has probably suffered more than any national capital in Europe. The streets are still filled with litter; people are barefoot and in rags and many are begging. I began by giving to each one, but soon realized this could not be as there are so many.

Fruit, cigarettes, and hardware are for sale on the street by peddlers, but prices are so high most people cannot buy. Many are calling "Americanski cigarette" — they are $2.50 per package.

As one walks about the city, the most sickening odors meet you from debris, dead bodies in the ruins, and filth. The sidewalks and streets are torn up in many places, and because of the lack of sanitary facilities, the people generally are filthy. It is indeed a sorry sight.

There is no service worthy of the name available anywhere. Cripples are everywhere and the terrors of war on every side. The feeling becomes so depressing on the streets, and one feels so helpless amidst it all that you find yourself wanting to leave or shut yourself from it in your room, poor though it be.

When we walk down the street, well-dressed and with U.S. pins, everyone stares at us and turns around and looks back at us as we walk on. The terrors of war will never be fully told. (ETB Journal.)

WEDNESDAY, JULY 31, 1946:
WARSAW, POLAND

Saw embassy officials this morning. Had satisfactory conference with Polish Minister of Justice. Although the

While in Poland President Benson used various forms of transportation, including this Polish *droshka*.

interpreter did a poor job both with English and German, we were able to make ourselves understood. He said Poland would welcome us in if we decide to establish a mission and declared that Poland wanted full religious freedom. He asked me to outline our beliefs and practices, organization, etc., which I did and promised to send him a Book of Mormon and other literature. (ETB Journal.)

We secured permission to visit Breslau in Silesia, where we have nearly 100 members remaining. Plane reservations could not be secured as planned, so Elders Gasser and Babbel left by overnight train Wednesday evening. They reported that the train trip was most revealing. All cars except one were horribly dirty freight cars into which people were jammed beyond capacity—women with babies, expectant mothers, men, women, and children—with all their belongings. Everyone looked so dirty and ragged. It was sickening to witness. People were piled on top of the cars, sticking out of the doors, standing outside between the cars, and it rained nearly all night. There were no facilities of any kind nor any water. People were forced to discard decency and privacy. (European Mission History.)

THURSDAY, AUGUST 1, 1946:
WARSAW AND BRESLAU, POLAND

Brothers Gasser and Babbel, who are traveling with me, left last night by train for Breslau. I remained for important conferences intending to take a plane; however, the travel bureau, the Polish airlines, and relief agencies were unable to get reservations. So I borrowed a jeep and driver and went early to the airport.

There I spoke to the man in charge, who fortunately could speak a little English. The Lord touched his heart, and he promised me I would get on although all seats were taken. I finally found myself in the plane sitting on a wooden stool instead of the wooden bench along the side of the plane. There were no safety belts, parachutes, or other equipment. I sat in the aisle until a Polish gentleman insisted I trade places with him. When it was evident resistance would avail nothing, I agreed.

We arrived in Breslau on a green, grassy runway after a one-and-one-half-hour trip. The brethren were not at the airport, so I walked up to a group of men busily talking and asked if anyone spoke English. A man who said he was a journalist came forward. I told him my desire to get to the city and to the address of the branch president. He wrote the Polish street name instead of the German one I had, introduced me to the president (mayor) of the city, and we started for the city in a car of ancient vintage, the gear of which kept slipping out about every five minutes.

He took me to the address of the branch president, where I greeted warmly some eight members huddled up in partly bombed-out buildings, none of whom could speak any English. They did make me understand a few things.

157

The brethren had been here but had left to return at 2:00 P.M. But they never returned.

After searching on the streets for someone who could speak English, I found a lady, with the help of the postman, and we got a few things straight. Later I visited the hall where we were to meet, also UNRA and the printing establishment of my journalist friend.

The meeting with some fifty Saints had just started when my lost brethren came in. We held a meeting with the Saints, learned of their conditions, gave what comfort and counsel we could, and then turned over relief supplies we'd brought with us and walked about three miles to our hotel.

There I got a private room with bath for which I am most grateful. (ETB Journal.)

Breslau has been nearly as badly damaged as Warsaw. The city is a shambles, swarming with displaced personnel from eastern Poland who have arrived here largely destitute, dirty, and hardly knowing where to go. Our Saints, who must now leave for the British Zone in Germany, are still carrying on bravely. Between the ruins of the building near their meetinghouse, which they have been able to keep through the long war years, they have planted a lovely garden and a potato patch which are assisting greatly in supplementing their meager food supply.

We met with forty-six of them in the evening and learned that living conditions here have been most deplorable. They have been subjected to slave labor, to plundering, rapine, and every manner of inhumane crime. To sustain life, they have been forced to sell what goods they have kept out of the hands of marauding bands, including their winter clothing—and, in many cases, everything except that which they had on their bodies. (European Mission History.)

Through the cooperation of the chief of the press association, announcements will be carried in all the large syndicated publications in an effort to locate our members wherever they may be in Poland so we might render them every assistance whether they remain in this land or find it necessary to be repatriated to Germany. Every effort is being made to assist those who remain and insure safety and security for those who are forced to leave. (European Mission History.)

Thanks so much for sending the pictures of you. They are grand. You get better looking all the time, and you don't look a day older. Don't you dare say again that you look old enough to be my father! (FAB to ETB.)

FRIDAY, AUGUST 2, 1946:
BRESLAU, KATOWICE, AND WARSAW, POLAND

Conference with local brethren in my room. Then went to city hall in Breslau and, although the outer office was full, was ushered in immediately to the office of the president (mayor) of the city. I had previously met him at the airport, and after explaining our purpose in visiting Poland, he assured us his full cooperation in giving our people special help in preparation for leaving and travel accommodations. I introduced him to our branch president, who will keep in touch and who left a list of our members for the president's use.

He invited me to stay over and ride with him to Katowice tomorrow, but because of appointments with government officials, I was unable to accept. But Brother Francis Gasser stayed behind to accept the offer.

Brother Babbel and I left by bus at 11:00 A.M. for Katowice, and after a rough ride on an overcrowded bus arrived at 4:40 P.M. After some checking on transportation, we accepted the invitation of a British UNRA official to ride to Warsaw with him. He kindly drove us to Gleiwitz, where we found a family of Saints with whom we left instructions and money and supplies. They will contact

159

the branch president in Breslau for details regarding moving and send a list to me in London. (ETB Journal.)

Then we accepted the invitation to ride in the station wagon to Warsaw. Although we had heard numerous stories of marauding bands who infested the highways at night, plundering, stealing and endangering life, we drove through the night without incident, being stopped only by military control posts several times along the way. (ETB Journal.)

SATURDAY, AUGUST 3, 1946:
WARSAW, POLAND

Arose late (9:00 A.M.) and after conferences with Ambassador Lane and others, I had a most pleasant visit with Poland's courageous democratic leader, Stanislaw Mikolajozuk, Vice-President and Minister of Agriculture for Poland. He assured me, among other things, of his full cooperation if we open a mission here.

Later I conferred with the new Minister of Labor and Public Welfare, who assured me of his help in locating our Saints and looking after their needs.

Later in the day I held a profitable conference with officials of the American Relief for Poland. (ETB Journal.)

SUNDAY, AUGUST 4, 1946:
WARSAW, POLAND, AND SELBONGEN, EAST PRUSSIA

We left by jeep (there was no other transportation available) for the southern half of East Prussia, which is now Poland, to try and locate and learn of the whereabouts of our members in that area.

We drove hard all day through rough roads and heavy rain in an army jeep. Several times we were directed in error, but finally we drove into the little cluster of homes where most of our Saints in the area live. (ETB Journal.)

Not a sign of life was upon the streets as we entered

the little village of Selbongen, East Prussia, in our faithful jeep. We thought it rather strange because it was a beautiful day to be out walking and enjoying the cool summer breezes. (European Mission History.)

The few Saints and children in view flew to cover as the jeep approached, fearing a repetition of experiences (which they related later) with soldiers. (ETB Journal.)

One sister tarried, and when she realized who I was, she exclaimed for joy and kissed my hands. Then she dashed to several homes, and in a very few seconds a roomful had assembled. Women and children and the one brother present broke into tears of joy, some of them out loud — so great was their happiness. Every few minutes others would be added. (ETB Journal.)

All was quiet as we entered the home of the branch president next door to the chapel, but as we were announced by the good sister whom we had met at the front of the chapel, women, children, and young girls appeared almost miraculously, crying and laughing excitedly and each trying to express as best they could the inexpressible joy that was theirs. Within a matter of moments, the cry went from one house to the next, "The Brethren are here," and soon we found ourselves surrounded by nearly fifty of the happiest people we have ever seen. Having seen the strange jeep approaching with what they feared to be either Polish or Russian soldiers, they had abandoned the streets as if by magic. Likewise when they learned of our identity and mission, the village became alive with joyous women and children — women and children because only two of the former twenty-nine priesthood members remain.

That morning in fast and testimony meeting over one hundred Saints had assembled together to bear their testimonies and to petition Almighty God in song, fasting, and prayer to be merciful unto them and let the missionaries again come to visit them. Our sudden and unheralded arrival, after almost complete isolation from Church and mission headquarters since early 1943, was the long-awaited answer to fasting and prayer—so wonderful that they could hardly believe their good fortune. Never have we seen love and gratitude more deeply expressed. Nothing could do but to have another meeting, and within an hour 104 members and friends were crowded into the plain but attractive chapel to enjoy the outpouring of the Spirit of the Lord in a most marvelous manner. (European Mission History.)

We greeted all warmly, and I gave fresh packages of gum to the children, which the children had never seen—sent by my never-failing wife. Although the Saints had held Sunday School and fast and testimony meeting, they all wanted us to hold one with them. Then they told how they'd fasted and prayed for the "Lord to send the Brethren," and that the theme today had been for contact with the Church.

We decided to meet at 6:30 P.M. as there are no lights available in either church or homes. There were 102 Saints and friends in the little church next to the branch president's home, and a sweet spirit prevailed.

While I was speaking, two armed soldiers entered the door at the front of the building in a most authoritative manner. The people were filled with fear, but the fear soon left them as I stopped long enough to motion them to a front seat, which they accepted somewhat reluctantly, as I went on telling of our activities in Europe, conferences with national and military officials in various nations, including Poland, our belief in freedom, liberty, and the basic principles of democracy. They were most attentive during my entire talk and also the brief talks of my associates which followed.

The Saints were overjoyed at the outcome, and after

162

the soldiers left we all sang and prayed and I gave them some final instruction.

Later in the home of the branch president, after shaking hands with all present, we visited further and we ate from their scanty store of food augmented somewhat by food we'd brought with us. Then again we listened to the most harrowing accounts of the dastardly deeds of soldiers on the members of this branch as a part of the German population of East Prussia.

Women and even little girls twelve years of age were ravaged as fiends in human form abused and raped these innocent faithful souls. Cases were reported where as many as ten soldiers, one after the other, forced relations with young girls of the branch—and in some cases while parents looked on at the point of a bayonet or were forcibly held by brutal soldiers. Never in all my life have I heard of such terrors, many of which included cold-blooded murder of husbands as their wives looked on helplessly.

No wonder the people acted like hunted fugitives. They've been plundered and robbed so many times that they have learned to secretly hide food, clothing, etc. Women and girls wore old-fashioned clothes, let their hair go unkempt and even their faces and homes dirty so as to be as uninviting as possible to the soldiers. (ETB Journal.)

Since the end of hostilities, our Saints have become a despised, persecuted and unwanted people because of their nationality. They have endured the most shocking and unspeakable cruelties and bestialities. One of the faithful brethren was shot down in cold blood by the invading troops from the East because he could not produce the cigarettes for which they had asked him. His mother, who ran to lift up his lifeless body from the pool of blood in which it lay, was driven away at the point of bayonets and threatened with death. As this forlorn mother comforted his grief-stricken wife—the mother of two lovely children— these soldiers whipped and flogged them so severely they

163

were unable to lie down for two weeks. Since that day women and girls, some of them just approaching adolescence, have been repeatedly ravished.

One of the sisters, whose husband was snatched from his sickbed of six weeks and deported to Siberia—a cripple on crutches and a semi-invalid for some time—was ravished three times in one night after having her home plundered, resulting in the birth of a little baby boy for whom she is now caring along with her two former children.

Until some two months ago they stood in daily fear of their lives; their homes were repeatedly entered at night and plundered. Everything the marauders desired was confiscated; their lusts ran rampant. Men, women, and children were taken from their homes never to be seen again.

When the armies withdrew in favor of the Poles, practically all cattle, horses, sheep, hogs, and fowl were taken with them. Remaining livestock was scarce and each family had one or two chickens, many of which have since been confiscated. Nearly the total egg production has been required by the occupying forces, and the present shortage of feed makes it questionable whether remaining poultry can be kept alive.

At one time the people found ingenious means for retaining the few remaining chickens. They placed them in watertight metal containers, weighed them down with stones, and placed them in the lake, going at night to bring them up to feed them, to replenish their air supply, and gather the occasional eggs which they laid. During the winter they found it necessary to cut holes through the ice in order to take care of their poultry.

Clothing and valuables were being ruthlessly confiscated as well. Many of the people dug up the sod and buried their belongings in shallow containers under the sod which they replaced. When such hiding places were discovered, the military went from place to place with long

164

sharp metal probing rods to locate hidden articles, most of which had been removed after the first alarm.

Most German men and women are forced to work eight to twelve hours a day, many of them receiving no pay or meals. Those who receive pay get the equivalent of forty cents per day (ten cents on the black market) for their labors. Women are required to work on road construction crews, as railroad section hands, as lumberjacks, or in jobs where filth and disease are ever present.

Our people have been forced to sell nearly all of their belongings, their winter clothes, their jewelry, etc., in order to sustain life. Ration cards allowing people to buy certain articles at regular prices have not been honored, necessitating purchasing food and other items at exorbitant prices on the black market.

Our Saints are facing a most critical period. One brother, after being repeatedly plundered, was again accosted for further plunder. When they learned that the coat and pants he was wearing had been given him by a friend to cover his nakedness following the last plundering in which everything had been taken and that he was wearing a woman's slip as a shirt—also borrowed—they felt rather ashamed and have since left him alone.

These are but a few of the innocent victims of war. The victorious armies, ever mindful of the inhuman atrocities which their loved ones had suffered during the long war years at the hands of the aggressor, their hearts now filled with hatred and the spirit of revenge, became fiends in human form and sought to justify their own villainous and cowardly acts by reason of the inhuman treatment meted out by their enemies during the conflict.

With the reestablishment of national boundaries, millions of people were required to seek homes elsewhere and are today milling around as homeless, displaced persons, fearful for their lives and despairing of the future. They are striving to avert death by starvation in the hope that

165

they may soon be repatriated and find a measure of security once more.

Most of our members in this community own their own lands and homes. The lands have been turned over to the Polish people coming into this territory, and all of the homes will subsequently be conscripted and confiscated as soon as the German people can be removed — all without one cent of money being paid in exchange for them. Some of the Saints still have retained a couple of small pieces of land on which they are raising potatoes and rye. They plant, grow, harvest, thresh, and grind the rye and then use it for bread. Particles of the grinding stones used were in evidence in the bread we ate.

This branch has carried on regular meetings through-out the entire war years with one or two brief interruptions. Twenty-five of the male membership are missing as prisoners of war. The two remaining brethren are doing a splendid job of trying to keep up the spirit of unity and love among the Saints and have succeeded marvelously.

Their faith and devotion today should be a testimony and an inspiration to the entire Church. The murdered brother is buried in a grave by the side of the chapel and the Saints are keeping it decked with flowers. I visited the grave in the cool of the morning and dedicated it. (European Mission History.)

After visiting this once beautiful city, it is easy to understand why it is considered the most devastated city in Europe. The buildings have all been gutted out by fire, thousands have been reduced to rubble, and the large ghetto area is completely leveled to the ground. The ruin and desolation are so complete that one cannot adequately describe it, nor does one desire to do so.

Poverty, disease, and filth are most apparent. The streets are terribly dirty, many of the people are in rags, walking barefooted, looking badly in need of bathing and sanitation. Yet the stores which are open and the streets and marketplaces are displayed with large quantities of all kinds of good food and every imaginable commodity and luxury.

Much of what is available is sold on the black market openly at outrageous prices. The average earnings of the people here are so small that hunger and starvation stalk in an agricultural land producing an abundant supply of food and other commodities. We were told repeatedly that normally a person can buy anything he wished in Warsaw if he had the price. American cigarettes are sold on the streets by scores of small boys and girls and old men and women at black market prices. Many of the food items for sale are from army stocks, and often these items, received through charitable institutions, are sold in order to secure sufficient funds to buy potatoes and bread — the two staple food items of the population.

During our stay in Poland we were shown every courtesy and the various governmental officials whom we visited were most cordial in their invitations extended to us and in their desire and willingness to assist us with the Church program in this nation. We were informed that religious freedom has now been established and the people are fighting desperately to retain it. The Polish people love freedom and liberty, but have been under domination so long in religion and politics that they rather fear to express themselves freely. (European Mission History.)

I am sitting in a small room in the upper part of the Polonia Hotel. There are three cots in the room, two of which hold Brother Babbel and the night watchman, both sound asleep. The table on which I write is covered with papers, food packages, and personal effects and is the only one in the room.

As I look out of the three-story window across the narrow street into windows of a partly bombed tenement house, I see people stirring and others still asleep. Dish towels and other materials are hanging from the windows, and some items of food are sitting in the windows to catch the cool night air.

On the street below can be heard horses' feet on the cobblestone streets as they pull small and very old wagons and other vehicles along.

Off in the distance can be seen, as far as the eye can reach, the ruins of what was one of the gayest, richest, and wickedest cities in the world — the capital of Poland. Of all the cities in Europe which I have seen, this presents the saddest sight of destruction and contrasts. People are ragged, poor, and terribly filthy and dirty. Food and clothing are available and unrationed, but prices are so high and people so poor they cannot buy. Small children are everywhere on the street calling, *"Papyroiosa, Americanska, Papyroiosa,"* which means American cigarettes.

It is estimated that about 450,000 people live in the city although during the worst of the long war almost everyone left. Before the war 1,350,000 lived here, many of whom were rich and of whom 350,000 were Jews. During the war through Nazi efforts many Jews were brought here until there were 500,000 here, practically all of whom were killed when the Ghetto (their section) was completely destroyed after Hitler had forced the Jews to build a high stone wall fence with electric wires on top around the entire area with machine guns mounted on the walls. Then the Jews were robbed, ravished, beaten, bombed, and burned until not one house is standing or even an apartment. It is the most desolate sight imaginable. It is estimated that 200,000 bodies of the helpless people lie buried in the rubble. Before the war there were 3,250,000 Jews in Poland of which only 40,000 to 50,000 are alive today. The total Jewish population of Europe was 9,612,000 before the war of which 5,787,000 were slaughtered. Only 1.3 to 1.6 percent of all the Jews in once Nazi-occupied territories are alive today.

Well, sweetheart, I mustn't dwell longer on this sickening scene. I am, however, mailing you a book, *German Crimes in Poland,* just released by a special government

168

commission which has been investigating for a year. You use your best judgment as to how much you show the girls. The reading is worse than the pictures and I've read only a few pages. I haven't the heart to read more now as I reside in the midst of the beastly results. (ETB to FAB.)

This is my husband's birthday. I have been blessed with the finest, purest, dearest, most devoted, and loyal husband and sweetheart. I truly thank my Heavenly Father for him constantly and for his wonderful life of service and devotion he is rendering to God's children. (FAB Journal.)

May you enjoy a pleasant and happy birthday and may the Lord grant that both of us may have many, many more useful birthdays together upon this earth to spend that time which the Lord sees fit to give us in spreading the truths of His Church and helping others to live better and happier, more worthwhile lives. (FAB to ETB.)

TUESDAY, AUGUST 6, 1946:
WARSAW, POLAND, AND BERLIN, GERMANY

Conferences this morning in Warsaw with Ambassador Bliss Lane and the Ministers of Foreign Affairs and New Territories of the Polish government.

Boarded an army freight plane for Berlin and arrived after a pleasant trip except for a few minutes in an electric storm.

Had dinner at the quarters of Brother Francis Gasser and then attended the MIA session of servicemen and women at which I was presented with a lovely birthday cake.

Arrived at the lovely home of Brother and Sister Eugene Merrill.

Brother Merrill informed me he had just received a letter from home containing a clipping to the effect Brother Alma Sonne has been appointed to preside over the European Mission and that he will come as soon as he can make arrangments. Although it is a surprise, if true—and I had expected to continue for at least another four to six months—I will be pleased to turn over to him the pleasant responsibility of directing affairs in Europe for the Church.

I hope I'll be able to carry forward some of the plans projected for the next two or three months, but I'm sure all will work out for the best as the First Presidency may direct. The conditions of the last six months have been a bit rough and rugged, but the Lord has sustained me in a most remarkable way—for which I shall ever be grateful.

I can well imagine how happy my family will be. They have been most loyal and devoted. No man ever had more complete unity or support in any mission than I have received in this one. As my noble forebear Ezra T. Benson said of his families as the Saints were driven from Nauvoo in 1846 (100 years ago), "Never at any time did I hear a murmur from their lips," so can I say of mine. How I thank the Lord for them and for all His rich blessings. (ETB Journal.)

It was sad to see so many men under arms and so much idleness in [Poland]. These are not conducive to reconstruction, to sound political or moral habits and ideals.

Here is a nation whose struggle for survival will require the united efforts of its people, an effort which the strong leaders are endeavoring to bring into fulfilment.

The spirit of the people seems very conducive to missionary work, and many of the government leaders contacted expressed the hope that we would see fit to extend our activities as a Church into that land now that religious freedom is being granted. (European Mission History.)

Upon arriving in Berlin, I received the following wire from the First Presidency, dated July 27, 1946: "Announcement made today of Alma Sonne as your successor to preside over European Mission. Date of departure will be sent you later. The First Presidency." (European Mission History.)

WEDNESDAY, AUGUST 7, 1946:
WARSAW, POLAND, AND FRANKFURT, GERMANY

A day of conferences, including East German Mission presidency; Dr. Olsen, head of Religious Affairs Branch; Col. Hester, head of Food and Agriculture Branch; the Polish Ambassador, etc. The results have been most satisfying.

In the evening after dinner with the Merrills in their lovely villa, I was honored at a birthday party by the servicemen and women at the home of Brother Gasser. A huge birthday cake provided by the boys was the center of our refreshments. Later Brother Gasser presented me with a lovely set of field glasses. (ETB Journal.)

Had further conferences with the Polish Military Mission and secured permission for future trips into Poland.

The representative of the International Red Cross informed us of the present shipments of welfare supplies now arriving throughout Germany, and contacts with General Clay and other military government officials were most profitable.

This trip has endeared our appreciation of the gospel and has shown the great need for the gospel principles to be taught to the nations of the earth, that the basis for real freedom and liberty might be proclaimed and established among the honest in heart. Our Saints, who have been called upon to suffer so much, to endure so many hardships and cruelties, show in their sweet spirit, in their increased loyalty and devotion to the Church and its principles, that the gospel of Jesus Christ brings to men and women the true peace, the true freedom and liberty for which the world is so desperately seeking. (European Mission History.)

The Religious Affairs Branch is becoming increasingly important to us in our work in Germany. Dr. C. Arild Olsen, a former associate in the cooperative movement in the USA, heads this important branch of OMGUS. He has a very sane approach to the religious problems in Germany and has been most friendly and helpful to us since his arrival here some two or three months ago. He and the members of his staff are doing all they can to increase the recognition on the part of General Clay and others of the importance which the Church can play in the reconstruction of Germany. Dr. Olsen favors the admission of mission presidents and missionaries, but to date his views have not prevailed, although I feel confident that this branch is making headway with its recommendations.

While I was in his office, word came from General Clay that approval had been given to the appointment of three permanent representatives of the three major religious groups—viz., Catholic, Protestant, and Jewish. He expressed his pleasure that I had been given permission to travel in the occupied areas, a privilege apparently not enjoyed by representatives of other faiths. Dr. Olsen feels confident that if we are persistent but patient we shall receive the permission we seek for mission presidents to be admitted for supervision of the work in the two German missions. (European Mission History.)

In Germany, as in several other European countries, the Church has not been recognized on an equal basis with other denominations. This lack of recognition has proven to be a great disadvantage in many instances and is generally unfavorable to the best progress of our work. I was assured today, however, that the four occupying powers have mutually agreed that in the future all religious organizations will be recognized on an equal basis and that complete religious freedom will be guaranteed. Our local brethren, who have labored under the old policy of discrimination, are delighted with the decision. Of course, only time and experience will determine whether it will work out as we hopefully expect. (European Mission History.)

In our visits with leaders of the Polish government, it was quite evident that the Polish people are determined to have complete religious freedom in the future. They were quite outspoken in their satisfaction that the Concordat between Rome and the Polish government has been broken and that in the future all churches will be on an equal basis throughout the nation. They offered every encouragement for us to establish a mission, and I was pleased to learn that several of them were somewhat familiar with our Church program. They seemed somewhat disappointed to learn that practically all of our membership in Poland today are German nationals.

We came away from Poland with the strong impression that now would be an opportune time to consider the establishment of a regular mission in that land. The people seem hungry for something that will satisfy their yearnings, and many of them seem disappointed in the failure of the dominant church to meet the needs of the people in spite of their strong hold on the religious and political life of the nation. (European Mission History.)

THURSDAY, AUGUST 8, 1946:
FRANKFURT, GERMANY

Last night, in dream, I was privileged to spend what seemed about an hour with President George Albert Smith in Salt Lake. It was a most impressive and soul-satisfying experience. We talked intimately together about the great work in which we are engaged and about my devoted family. I felt the warmth of his embrace as we both shed tears of gratitude for the rich blessings of the Lord.

I love this great and good man — a friend of all God's children. The last day or so I have been wondering if my labors in Europe have been acceptable to the First Presi-

173

dency and the Brethren at home and especially to my Heavenly Father. This sweet experience has tended to put my mind completely at ease, for which I am deeply grateful. (ETB Journal.)

FRIDAY, AUGUST 9, 1946:
FRANKFURT, GERMANY

Went to the airport preparatory to leaving for London, but after three hours of waiting the flight was cancelled on account of bad weather. As there were no other means of travel available, we returned to the hotel and did some reading and writing for the balance of the afternoon. (ETB Journal.)

Darling, how I miss you and the children and long for the time when I can see you again. I am so grateful we've been able to come here to offer a little help to these poor people. Their needs are great. How the terrors of war have torn people from their moorings and brought untold suffering. How thankful I am my family are in the good old USA—a land choice above all others. The people stop and stare at us as we go anywhere. We are admired and wondered at—the marvel of the world is the USA. (ETB to FAB.)

SATURDAY, AUGUST 10, 1946:
FRANKFURT, GERMANY, AND PARIS, FRANCE

Left for Paris enroute to London. Arrived in Paris, but stormy weather again delayed our flight and we were taken to Paris for the night.

Spent the afternoon visiting the Arch de Triumph and Louvre Art Gallery—a most enjoyable and profitable experience. It was especially impressive to view the city from atop the arch. The lovely field glasses given me in Berlin were greatly enjoyed. (ETB Journal.)

SUNDAY, AUGUST 11, 1946:
PARIS, FRANCE, AND LONDON, ENGLAND

I cabled the First Presidency as follows: Just received wire regarding successor. Surprised but it's all right. Believe it important I remain at least until Sonne arrives and complete September schedule and another visit to Poland. (European Mission History.)

Today was most glorious because our wonderful husband and father called from London, England, over the telephone. He sounded tired in his dear voice but, oh, so sweet and dear. He talked to all six children.

He told of receiving his letter of release as president of the European Mission. It will still be necessary that he stay until Brother Sonne arrives, which will be two or three months, and then the Presidency of the Church want him to stay and explain and help Brother Sonne get on to the work that he has accomplished with hard work and the help of our Heavenly Father. My husband has done a most magnificent work in Europe helping our Church people and others. (FAB Journal.)

TUESDAY, AUGUST 13, 1946:
LONDON, ENGLAND

Office all day. Dinner at British Mission home and then played ball with members of the London Branch on the Wandsworth Common Green. I was amused at the surprise of the Saints when during the game, in four times at the bat, I made four hits and three runs. It was a pleasant diversion. (ETB Journal.)

THURSDAY, AUGUST 15, 1946:
LONDON, ENGLAND, AMSTERDAM, NETHERLANDS,
AND GENEVA, SWITZERLAND

Left London for Geneva. Stopped for two hours in Amsterdam and had pleasant conference with President Cornelius Zappey of the Netherlands Mission. Left for

175

President Benson and Max Zimmer inspect welfare supplies from the United States that had arrived in Geneva, Switzerland.

Geneva, but returned to airport because of a bad motor. Took off again in fifteen minutes but the second plane returned to the field because of a defective radio. The third time was a success, after I'd joshed the KLM officials about providing us with horses, and we arrived at Geneva. (ETB Journal.)

FRIDAY, AUGUST 16, 1946:
GENEVA, SWITZERLAND

Conferences with International Red Cross officials and inspection of our welfare supplies in the warehouses in the morning. I then prepared instructions regarding distribution into Germany and Austria and in the afternoon held another conference with officials of Red Cross and completed all arrangements for future handling of our welfare products. It surely seemed good to see these large quantities of food, clothing, and bedding here for our Saints in good containers, well preserved, and in good storehouses. I hope and pray it reaches those so sorely in need without undue delay. (ETB Journal.)

176

To date the equivalent of sixteen carloads of foodstuffs and seven carloads of clothing have arrived for distribution in these stricken areas. In addition, welfare supplies in volume have arrived for our Saints in Norway, Holland, Belgium, France, and Czechoslovakia and parcel post packages of food and clothing for these and other missions in Europe outside the occupied areas. (European Mission History.)

The Church welfare supplies have arrived in good condition and are neatly stored and properly catalogued in the modern and spacious warehouses of the International Red Cross at Geneva. These supplies were inspected and all inventories carefully checked, loaded, and unloaded entirely within these enclosures. A large staff of trained men insures every precaution being taken for efficient and expeditious handling of all supplies in accordance with the schedule agreed upon.

On the basis of this schedule, approximately ten percent of our present welfare stocks will be shipped with each succeeding train scheduled to move about once per month into the occupied areas. Distribution will be based on fifty-seven percent for the West German Mission, thirty-six percent for the East German Mission and seven percent for Austria. Each shipment is to include some of each commodity in our total stocks, made up in approximately the same proportion. The officials of the organization are cooperating wholeheartedly and are doing a splendid job of following through on all the details. (European Mission History.)

SATURDAY, AUGUST 17, 1946:
GENEVA, SWITZERLAND

In Geneva all day alone. Brother Zimmer left for Basel last night. Further conferences and work in my room. Also walked about the city and heard the symphony for an hour in the park. (ETB Journal.)

The cost of living has gone up terribly. Children's clothes and other things are very high. Groceries and foodstuffs are simply outrageous. Eggs are seventy cents a dozen, butter eighty cents a pound, milk is real high, and everything is climbing up fast. (FAB to ETB.)

TUESDAY, AUGUST 20, 1946:
ZURICH, SWITZERLAND

Spent the day with President Taggart regarding mission problems. Made careful inspection of mission home and authorized considerable needed repairs and renovation inside and out.

Left for Paris by train sharing a sleeping compartment with a cigar-smoking Hebrew. He was cordial and I had a fairly restful night. (ETB Journal.)

WEDNESDAY, AUGUST 21, 1946:
PARIS, FRANCE, AND LONDON, ENGLAND

Arrived in London. Was happy to find sweet letters from my wife telling that all is well at home. (ETB Journal.)

FRIDAY, AUGUST 23, 1946:
LONDON, ENGLAND

Met in missionary meeting with sixteen newly arrived missionaries and others at British Mission headquarters.

Afternoon spent in office. Wired the First Presidency regarding definite advice on proposed trip to Palestine-Syrian and South African missions. I have been anxious to go, if they approve, because our Saints in Syria are faced with the necessity of moving in body to Armenia which is now in the Soviet Union. We, of course, will be guided by the decision of the First Presidency. (ETB Journal.)

SUNDAY, AUGUST 25, 1946:
LONDON, ENGLAND

All day important mission work at the office. Attended the evening session of the branch conference of the St.

Albans Branch near London. Spoke forty-five minutes with great freedom. There was a sweet spirit present for which I was deeply grateful. (ETB Journal.)

Have just had our little dinner, which made me think again of your constant kindness because most of the meal was from things you sent—tuna, bouillon, and candy. Thanks for all the things you've sent and done! (ETB to FAB.)

It's cold in London today. I have the electric heater going full blast in my room. As I enjoy my cozy little bedroom-office, the photo of my lovely wife and children looks down at me, and once or twice during the day I've looked through the leather folder at all the pictures. These make you all seem a bit closer, but not nearly close enough. (ETB to FAB.)

MONDAY, AUGUST 26, 1946:
LONDON, ENGLAND

Arose and wrote my devoted and ever-faithful wife as I aim to do at least twice each week. My gratitude for her and the children increases with the passing weeks. Always loyal, unselfish, and understanding, I prize her love and companionship more each day. She is a true and fully worthy companion who in every respect puts the Church first and her husband and family before all else.

No man could ask for more than I have in the "choice companion for the journey of life" which was promised me in my patriarchal blessing on my return from my first mission in December 1923. This has been fully fulfilled as have all other promises made in my two blessings. How I thank my Heavenly Father for it all. May I increase in worthiness for all His rich blessings. I marvel ofttimes that I have been so richly blessed—if I can only remain ever true and faithful, which I pray for daily.

Wrote a joint letter to my ten brothers and sisters today.

Time does not permit, now at least, personal correspondence with each one even though I would enjoy such. It was a joy to write them. (ETB Journal.)

THURSDAY, AUGUST 29, 1946:
LONDON, ENGLAND

London office and at British Mission headquarters checking on European library and the history of our work in Europe. Evening spent dictating letters. (ETB Journal.)

Went to the temple this evening and helped with sealings for the dead on the Benson lines — thirty-five couples and one hundred forty-nine children. The evening was most glorious. It would have been perfect if you could have been present. (FAB to ETB.)

SATURDAY, AUGUST 31, 1946:
LONDON, ENGLAND, AND GOTEBORG, SWEDEN

Left office for Goteborg. Wrote letters enroute to my children. Met by President Eben R.T. Blomquist and missionaries and Saints. Inspected three prospective buildings for chapels as no materials are available for building. Attended meeting with Saints and friends — 80 present. Then, after a cup of Postum, retired on a Swedish pullman at 11 P.M. (ETB Journal.)

This trip to attend the Food and Agricultural Organization (FAO) conference was made in conjunction with a scheduled visit of the three Scandinavian missions. (European Mission History.)

MONDAY, SEPTEMBER 2, 1946:
MALMO, SWEDEN, AND COPENHAGEN, DENMARK

Left Malmo by boat and arrived in Copenhagen.

After checking in at the mission home went direct to FAO meetings. This is the conference of the FAO of the United Nations Organization. At the request of the USA delegation, I spoke to the group in the evening regarding my observations in Europe. (ETB Journal.)

TUESDAY, SEPTEMBER 3, 1946:
COPENHAGEN, DENMARK

Meetings of FAO all day. Made several acquaintances and received old friendships from the London IFAP Conference of last June. In evening took dinner with some of the Saints. President Petersen accompanied me. (ETB Journal.)

As I sit in the first row balcony near the chairman in the FAO meeting convened in the beautiful Christiansborg Palace, my thoughts turn to you, sweetheart.

The conference, attended by representatives of 30 nations with many others represented by observers, is conducted in English and French so when the French translation is being given I have little in the conference to hold my attention. Of course, I realize that, with so many nations represented, two languages at least are necessary.

This is possibly Denmark's most lovely building which is adapted so well to a world conference of this kind. I am mixing in a good bit of church work, and look upon my attendance primarily as a missionary endeavor.

Last night, at the invitation of our USA delegation, I spoke to them regarding my observations in Europe. We were together for four hours and the last one-and-a-half hours were spent discussing spiritual and moral problems and our Church. I am most grateful for the opportunity which was provided.

Today I guided some of the USA group to see the famous Thorvaldsen's Museum and the Frue Kirke (Church) where the Christ and Twelve Apostles, done in marble by this world-famous sculptor 100 years ago, are located. (ETB to FAB.)

I went and canned corn at the Church Welfare Square until two o'clock in the morning. (FAB Journal.)

181

President Benson attended the Conference of the United Nations Food and Agricultural Organization held in the luxurious Kristianborg Castle in Copenhagen.

THURSDAY, SEPTEMBER 5, 1946:
COPENHAGEN, DENMARK, AND MALMO, SWEDEN

FAO meetings. Also attended a meeting of the executive committee of the IFAO created last June in London. Conferred with Presidents Petersen and West.

Left Copenhagen by train and later took boat to Malmo, Sweden, where I took midnight sleeper for Stockholm. (ETB Journal.)

FRIDAY, SEPTEMBER 6, 1946:
STOCKHOLM, SWEDEN

Arrived in Stockholm and spent the day conferring with President Blomquist, visiting with President and Sister Cowles, missionaries, and friends and in taking care of mail and inspecting three prospective mission home buildings.

Attended meeting of the Saints and spoke for forty-five minutes on the children of Judah, which question is

182

very much in the news today. Many people, nations, and prominent Jews are opposing the return of Judah to Palestine. The spirit of gathering is resting so powerfully upon them that they are flocking to that land under the most adverse circumstances resulting in much suffering. Of course it is all in fulfillment of prophecy in the Bible, Book of Mormon, and Doctrine and Covenants, and no matter what nations or individuals say or do, the Jews will return to Palestine.

Left for Oslo on sleeper. A large group of Saints were at the station with gifts of food, flowers, etc., and sang a sweet farewell.

In the meeting they presented me with a lovely pair of sterling silver candlestick holders for my wife and me. I shall never forget their love and kindness. (ETB Journal.)

SATURDAY, SEPTEMBER 7, 1946:
OSLO, NORWAY

Arrived in Oslo. Met at the station by President A. Richard Peterson and several missionaries. After breakfast at the mission home office, we drove to Drammen — some 20 miles — to inspect the building now being rented but which will soon be offered for sale. I found the building quite undesirable both as to location and condition and advised the brethren against purchase but encouraged them to locate a suitable lot in a desirable part of the city and plan to build in keeping with our needs and Church policy.

In the evening I addressed a large meeting of the Relief Society and the priesthood in Oslo. (ETB Journal.)

One of the truly unforgettable experiences of a visitor to the services of the Oslo Branch in Norway is the memory of the delightful singing of the famous Oslo Choir and the stirring music of the equally talented orchestra. Missionaries for many years have thrilled to their artistry and have returned home loudly singing their praises. Today they are the pride of the Scandinavian missions.

According to information received through old reports, the choir was organized on January 31, 1856. Today it has seventy members, and its leader, Ramm Arveseter, has been conducting for the last fifteen years. Sister Mary Nielson has been its organist for the past twenty-three years.

The choir, in additon to rendering musical numbers for every Sunday evening service, holds two concerts yearly. These concerts have become traditional, and the attendance fills the chapel to overflowing. The choir has also made a practice of visiting various hospitals from time to time to sing for the patients. At the present time the choir is preparing for its ninetieth jubilee, which will be held this fall.

The Oslo Branch orchestra was organized on November 20, 1944, under the auspices of Ramm Arveseter, Brother Alf Johansen being selected as its supervisor. The orchestra's aim was not only to assist in accompanying the choir but also to stimulate musical interests among the Saints. It now consists of seventeen active members. One of their former members, Brother Eric Brunn, was a leader of the Norwegian underground during the war. Upon being discovered, he was shot to death, his body thrown in the ocean and never recovered.

These two outstanding musical organizations, products of a mission branch, should be a challenge to the entire Church membership and an inspiration as well. What they have done and are continuing to do might well be duplicated in other missions, wards, and stakes throughout the Church. (European Mission History.)

MONDAY, SEPTEMBER 9, 1946:
OSLO, NORWAY, AND LONDON, ENGLAND

Left Oslo via American Overseas Airlines and arrived at Croydon, London. Reached my office and found my desk piled high with mail. Many difficult problems are awaiting my attention which I pray the Lord will direct me in meeting. (ETB Journal.)

TUESDAY, SEPTEMBER 10, 1946:
LONDON, ENGLAND

Arose at 6:00 A.M. on the twentieth anniversary of my happy marriage. It has seemed a short twenty years. They have been most happy and filled with activity.

I have been given a choice companion for the journey of life. My loving and devoted wife, Flora, has been all I could ever ask for in a faithful and loyal companion.

As I arose this morning, I thanked the Lord for her as I am wont to do each day. As a mother, I never have seen her superior. She is all, I am sure, that the Lord expects in Latter-day Saint motherhood.

Spent the day at the office dictating and talking on long distance phone. Three or four times during the day Brother Arthur Butler sang a group of lovely songs which I have asked him to sing to my wife and children as an expression of my love for them and our sweet and sacred home life.

I was overjoyed to hear the voices of my wife and six children as I spoke to them over the telephone in my home in Salt Lake City for five minutes.

It has been a pleasant soul-satisfying day, although I have missed my lovely and ever-true companion and children. God bless them all at home. (ETB Journal.)

I love you with all my heart and ever miss you and long for you. Sometimes I wonder what people do who are separated from their wives and not engaged in the work of the Lord. It must be terrible, or else they don't love their wives like I do mine. (ETB to FAB.)

This day is the most important day to me, along with the day I was born. The reason it is the most glorious and wonderful day to me is because twenty years ago I had the privilege of marrying the grandest companion and husband. Today is our wedding anniversary.

My darling, ever-thoughtful husband called me from London, England, at twelve o'clock today. It was most glorious to talk to him. I love and adore him more than life itself. I would do all within my power and strength to make my husband successful and happy. He is so wonderful, capable, and good.

He had two dozen of the Beauty red roses sent to me today and a card saying the following on it: "To my darling wife and sweetheart, Flora, on the twentieth anniversary of the happiest day of my life. You have made the past twenty years the happiest and yet seem the shortest imaginable. Since the day I first saw you, I have loved you. That love, through our years of courtship, interrupted by two missions, and happy marriage, has become deeper and more sacred. God bless you. With all my love and affection, T." (FAB Journal.)

This evening President George Albert Smith came to our home and made a nice, cheerful, and pleasant visit on our family. I did appreciate it so very much.

He told of the wonderful work my husband was doing. He said I deserved a vacation, and he thought it would be fine if I could meet my husband when he came home from Europe. He said he was going to write my husband in the morning. (FAB Journal.)

FRIDAY, SEPTEMBER 13, 1946:
LONDON, ENGLAND

Early dictation. Received call that President Boyer had been hit by a car while crossing the intersection near the British Mission headquarters enroute to the train. I rushed to the hospital, administered to him, and arranged for his care. After being assured by the physician that he would X-ray his head because of pain there, but that he would be all right, I returned to my quarters for a conference with cooperative leaders enroute to Zurich to attend a meeting of coop leaders sponsored by the International Cooperative

Alliance. Helped them a bit regarding travel and economic questions pertaining to Europe. (ETB Journal.)

I know you are under a great strain, and I wish so much I could do something to help relieve you of part of your heavy load. It worries me, dear. You are such a hard worker and so courageous. Isn't it possible to get a little help in the home, to eat out a bit more, or something? Please spare yourself all you can. (ETB to FAB.)

SATURDAY, SEPTEMBER 14, 1946:
LONDON, ENGLAND, AND FRANKFURT, GERMANY

Left London for Frankfurt. Arrived in Frankfurt just late enough to miss my connection for Berlin.

Checked in at the Carlton Hotel (army officers), and fortunately the German girl at the desk remembered the call from General Lucius D. Clay's office in Berlin reserving rooms for me on my last visit, so I was spared the trouble of going to the billeting office and taking a chance of being unable to get quarters or getting less comfortable ones.

Went to booking office and got reservations for Berlin. Called our LDS servicemen's group to tell them I wouldn't be there and learned they had planned open house tonight honoring me with printed programs, orchestra, etc. Am very sorry we are all disappointed.

Spent evening working in my room. Following dinner, I walked through the city for an hour. Ruin is everywhere. My heart became so heavy as I walked through streets lined with rubble and bombed and burned buildings that I found myself silently shedding tears of sorrow.

Then my attention would be attracted to old men, young men, and boys following smoking U.S. soldiers waiting for them to throw the cigarette stub away so they could pick it up and either smoke it or, more commonly, put it out and then slip it in their pockets to be rerolled later and used, or more than likely sold, on the black market.

187

Crude as it may seem, it reminded me of hogs following grain-fed steers in the feedlots of the Corn Belt, only in the latter case the scavengers received some food value while these human scavengers receive drugs that are harmful to the body but satisfy an artificially built-up craving habit.

My heart has seldom been so heavy as tonight as I contemplate the conditions of these war-torn countries and, in fact, the world as a whole. (ETB Journal.)

I am still hopeful it will be possible to go into Poland again, although the serviceman who was going with me has been refused permission, after former approval, because of the tense feeling in the Russian Zone and in Poland since Secretary Byrnes' speech a few days ago at Stuttgart. The people have been demonstrating in front of the U.S. Embassy in Warsaw, and five U.S. cars have been stolen in the Berlin area in the last few days — one of them a large new UNRRA vehicle.

We can tell better what to do when I arrive in Berlin and size up the situation. The head of the Polish Military Mission in Berlin has been very friendly to me in the past and assured me after my first trip he'd grant permission for additional visits. (ETB to FAB.)

As I sit in this comfortable room in a partially bombed hotel and look out of the window, I see destruction as far as the eye can reach.

Across the street in the rubble of a once beautiful building, men and women are trying to find a few little sticks of wood to carry home to cook their meager food. Occasionally an old man or woman, often with little barefooted children following, goes by pushing or pulling little old wagons or baby carriages with a few sticks which they've gathered out in the country.

I'm so grateful you and the children can be spared the views of the terrible ravages of war. I fear I'll never be able to erase them from my memory. The effect on little children must be terrible and so lasting. (ETB to FAB.)

MONDAY, SEPTEMBER 16, 1946:
BERLIN, GERMANY

Another meeting with mission presidency preceded by conference with President Ranglack. Later conferences with Polish Military Mission, Ambassador Murphy, Dr. Olsen, head of Religious Affairs Branch of OMGUS, et al.

Was happy to learn that the officials are finally coming to the view that church organizations should be allowed to distribute relief supplies directly to their people without pooling relief through a general relief agency. This is much more effective and will result in more total relief contributions. (ETB Journal.)

TUESDAY, SEPTEMBER 17, 1946:
BERLIN, GERMANY

Just a hurried note while waiting for my next appointment here in the Office of Military Government U.S. (OMGUS). I have just been to the finance office, where I was the first person to receive the new currency which goes into effect today with all the military U.S. forces in Germany. For three days everything has been closed for purchases or sales pending the changeover. The introduction of the new currency is an effort to control the black market. This money is different from what the Germans have, so the new money can be used only in military places. Of course this will not prevent Americans from buying cigarettes, etc., at the army store (PX) and exchanging them secretly for German articles on the black market, but there is a limit to the quantity of cigarettes, candy, etc., that each soldier can purchase.

Well, darling, I'm not going in to Poland. The authorities advise against it and the Polish military officials here seem to be against it. In fact, they've told me that I shouldn't have traveled freely in Poland contacting our

German Saints as I did before. For some good reason, I did not learn of their strict rules and so proceeded to do the work we needed to do and, after accomplishing our mission, reported to the authorities what we'd done.

When I talk with my good Polish friend here who is head of the Polish Military Mission, he tells me that the officials in Poland are surprised I traveled about the nation without being stopped—and apparently they are somewhat displeased. But as our Ambassador Murphy said to me yesterday, "Mr. Benson, it's fortunate for you, I suppose, that you were not familiar with all their restrictions or else you would not have been able to contact your people in Poland at all."

So again the Lord has worked things out for us in a most peculiar way, and all is well because most of our people are now out of Poland according to information received since coming into Germany. Our assistance was just in time.

Honey dear, it seems so different on this trip. For one thing the weather is lovely. The surroundings here at U.S. headquarters have been greatly improved, and many of the traces of war have been removed. However, when one goes into other parts of the city, all is destruction and poverty, and one soon has a feeling of sadness and despondency.

Although the condition of the people is somewhat improved, one of the serious matters is that there is as yet no fuel available for the Germans for the winter ahead. In our meeting yesterday with the acting mission presidency, they wrapped themselves in blankets because already the nights and mornings here are cold. Fortunately for the mission home, the brethren followed my suggestion this spring and cut down three huge trees to let in some sunlight for the garden and have cut them all up and have them stored under cover. This will be a great help during the coldest weather. (ETB to FAB.)

WEDNESDAY, SEPTEMBER 18, 1946:
BERLIN, GERMANY

More conferences with representatives of the same agencies as yesterday.

To my joy, I learned today of the arrival of large supplies of welfare products—clothing, food, and bedding. With President Ranglack of the East German Mission, following conferences with Red Cross officials, we visited the warehouses where our supplies are stored. They were all in good condition, and tomorrow, after submission of a plan for distribution to the Russian and local authorities, we hope to get approval for immediate distribution to our needy members.

Our hearts filled with deep gratitude as we gazed upon these lovely products of kind and unselfish LDS hands across the sea in Zion. (ETB Journal.)

THURSDAY, SEPTEMBER 19, 1946:
BERLIN, GERMANY

Appointments mission office. The local mission officers are delighted with the arrival today of 1,000 copies of the Book of Mormon shipped from Frankfurt.

Left for Frankfurt via overnight military train. Three minutes before the train left, a call went out over the loudspeaker for everyone going to Frankfurt to board the train as the doors would be locked and not unlocked until the train reached Frankfurt tomorrow morning.

I shared a compartment with a cigar-smoking Quaker. The ventilation being poor, I am not too happy. Will be pleased when we reach our destination. (ETB Journal.)

FRIDAY, SEPTEMBER 20, 1946:
FRANKFURT, GERMANY

No matter where I go—on land, on the sea, in the air, or amid the horrors of war—my thoughts frequently turn to you, my dear, whom I love so dearly. All I have seen and experienced but increases my gratitude and affection for you.

It is such a joy to hold you in my thoughts and contemplate the time when I'm to be with you again.

Last night on the train—my first ride on the "Berliner" (a military train from Berlin to Frankfurt)—I found myself longing for you to make the trip with me. (ETB to FAB.)

SATURDAY, SEPTEMBER 21, 1946:
FRANKFURT, GERMANY, AND LONDON, ENGLAND

Left hotel. Heavy storm during night at airport had leveled some barracks, blown down all power lines, and knocked several planes around. Each plane had to be flight tested before any official flights left. In all, we took off at 11:30 A.M. instead of 8:00 A.M. as scheduled. Then we stopped in ten minutes at Wiesbaden to check finally on weather.

After some little delay, we took off for what proved the roughest trip yet. (ETB Journal.)

The plane was loaded with G.I.s and some German prisoners. I was the only civilian. We sat on regular bucket seats used in planes to transport troops during the war. That was not so bad, as I've done it scores of times, but the man guarding the prisoners got sick and let go on the metal floor. The odor almost made others sick. Well, it's over and my stomach didn't act up a bit, for which I'm grateful. (ETB to FAB.)

However, in due course we arrived at London and the flat to find my desk piled high with mail.

It is a joy to have three choice letters from my ever-devoted and faithful wife. How I love her and thank the Lord for her constantly. She gives me word that Elder Alma Sonne will leave New York City by boat for Europe October 14 and should arrive here about October 20.

My darling Flora—although I know she'd love to join

me in Europe—is so unselfishly understanding and emphasizes so sweetly that she will be more than pleased to meet me here, in New York City, or at home as the Brethren and I advise. She has been so closely tied at home and worked so hard for so long that she surely more than deserves a real vacation. Yet she never complains but works unceasingly and loyally supports me in all my labors, for which I am most thankful although not fully worthy, I fear, of such rich blessings. (ETB Journal.)

SUNDAY, SEPTEMBER 22, 1946:
LONDON, ENGLAND

The call I placed for my dear wife yesterday has been delayed because of weather interference. I have been so anxious to complete the call so we can decide definitely where and about when Flora should meet me. I have prayed she would feel as I and would not be disappointed. We have always seen eye to eye, and I'm sure, living as close to the Lord as she does, her impressions will be as mine are. Will hope the call may come through—although it's now twelve o'clock midnight and the prospects aren't very good. (ETB Journal.)

MONDAY, SEPTEMBER 23, 1946:
LONDON, ENGLAND

At two o'clock this morning the call came through. The reception was very good.

I was made grateful to learn from my dear companion that our impressions were the same—viz., that she should not come to Europe at this time. It was a sweet experience to talk to her for six minutes. We are so very happy and grateful for the prospects of meeting in New York City when the work is finished over here and enjoy a few days together.

Worked at the office all day. Had two sisters from the British Mission help me as typists. There is so much mail. I dictated most of the day. (ETB Journal.)

TUESDAY, SEPTEMBER 24, 1946:
LONDON, ENGLAND

Office all day dictating and preparing bulletin to mission presidents. Had two sisters helping me again today. Received much mail, including a lovely letter from my sweetheart wife.

Called on President Boyer for an hour in the evening and found him up and much improved. (ETB Journal.)

WEDNESDAY, SEPTEMBER 25, 1946:
LONDON, ENGLAND; BRUSSELS, BELGIUM; GENEVA, SWITZERLAND

Left office for Brussels. Arrived in Brussels and was met by President and Sister James L. Barker of the French Mission, who had driven up from Paris to meet me and take care of other mission business. We had three hours together. We considered several mission problems. Among other things, I counseled him to secure a mission translator to translate literature for use in the mission and that President Barker arrange his time so he could prepare some tracts and pamphlets for submission to the mission literature committee aimed at the French and Catholic people. (ETB Journal.)

FRIDAY, SEPTEMBER 27, 1946:
BASEL, SWITZERLAND, AND ZURICH, SWITZERLAND

Conferences with President Zimmer and Taggart. Approved, after inspection, the purchase of 300 to 400 Swiss used army blankets for use of refugees and bombed-out Saints in West German Mission.

Went to train in evening with overnight train ticket, as I thought, to find that the 6:56 on the ticket was army time or morning.

Went back to the hotel, where I learned there are only three trains weekly, and fortunately got a room and began at once to check on transportation by air with a prayer in

194

my heart. Was given no encouragement on such short notice.

Finally Swissair called Zurich and got space for seven-thirty in the morning. Then the problem was to get to Zurich and, if I got there, to get hotel room. Took 7:30 P.M. train to Zurich and secured a hotel.

I am now in Zurich and in a comfortable room ready for a rest and to report at the Swissair offices at 6:30 A.M. tomorrow for Prague. Again I thank the Lord for opening the way. (ETB Journal.)

President George Albert Smith called and paid us a lovely visit to our home. He is so kind and thoughtful of me and our needs. He is a most busy gentleman, and his time is so valuable that I certainly feel it is a real honor for him to call on our family and me. (FAB Journal.)

SATURDAY, SEPTEMBER 28, 1946:
PRAGUE, CZECHOSLOVAKIA

An effort is being made to locate all of our Saints and visit them as rapidly as possible. A reorganization has been effected in the two branches at Prague and at Brno. Some of the old officers have been reappointed and many new people brought into activity. Plans are underway to open a third branch.

Brother Roubicek, former acting mission president and president of the Prague Branch, who has been deferred from military service twice on account of his Church responsibilities, is leaving this week to enter the military service for a period of five months as a part of the national military service program (compulsory). At the end of the five-month period he expects to return to his work at a local hotel in Prague.

The one-half car of clothing for this mission has arrived, and the one-half car of food which was lost has been located and is in Czechoslovakia, although it has not yet reached its destination in Prague. The American Relief for Czechoslovakia organization has agreed to provide satisfactory storage space free to the Church until our welfare supplies are distributed.

In view of the steady improvement of economic conditions in this nation, it is estimated that the two shipments of clothing and food will suffice to meet the needs of the Saints in this mission—at least for the foreseeable future.

Plans are underway for the organization of welfare food-producing projects in 1947. (European Mission History.)

SUNDAY, SEPTEMBER 29, 1946:
PRAGUE, CZECHOSLOVAKIA, AND LONDON, ENGLAND

Held public meeting with Saints and friends with a good attendance and sweet spirit present.

Following lunch, I reported to the airways terminal, according to the suggestion made to President Toronto a day or so before, in the hope I might get transportation back, as my work was finished—although there were twenty-eight on the waiting list ahead of me. The officials reported there was no possibility, but I felt somehow I was to leave on that plane and so had the lieutenant take me to the airport in his jeep.

On arrival there, I was informed there was no chance. However, I waited while the passengers checked through customs. Then, just as the plane was about to leave, the head official came out and told me he felt impressed to take off some diplomatic mail and make room for me. So in a few minutes we were on our way—one more evidence that the Lord is with His servants.

The four brethren, as I bade them good-bye, shook their heads in astonishment.

About three-and-one-half hours later we arrived at London in a dense fog. Three other planes were there ahead of us and still in the air although we could not see them. We circled the airport for twenty minutes, and then after one unsuccessful attempt to land finally made it with the aid of lights and flares. (ETB Journal.)

WEDNESDAY, OCTOBER 2, 1946:
LONDON, ENGLAND

Office all day attending to matters pertaining to the twelve missions in the European Mission. (ETB Journal.)

Our Saints, who generally speaking have lived the gospel, have been much more fortunate than their nonmember associates. In the first place, they have been recipients of the glorious blessings of living the Word of Wisdom. As a result, they do not have the enslaving habits of coffee, tea, tobacco, and liquor. Instead of trading food for these drugs, they have used their allotment to exchange for food.

They have had a more hopeful and optimistic outlook and have done more to help themselves. Our branches have been in an unusual degree fully united. Our people, as a whole, are frugal and careful with their means. They have sustained each other in the spirit of love and fellowship and have not dissipated their energies through worry, fear, bickering, and complaint. They have had valuable help through many loyal and devoted LDS servicemen and, of course, now they have the much-welcomed welfare supplies from Zion. (ETB to FAB.)

THURSDAY, OCTOBER 3, 1946:
LONDON, ENGLAND

Office until noon and then to airport to go to Paris. However, a combination of weather, defective cables, reporting conditions, and other delays made it unwise if not impossible for me to go, especially when one plane turned back at the Channel and we were informed that our plane may have to go into another airport and on to Paris tomorrow. The cost involved, the hazard involved, and the impression which I received against going made me decide not to wait longer at the airport. Returned to lodge and completed dictation. (ETB Journal.)

FRIDAY, OCTOBER 4, 1946:
LONDON, ENGLAND

Today the general conference of the Church convenes on Temple Square. How I miss being in attendance, and yet I know I'm where the Lord wants me and I'm happy and grateful to serve in any capacity or in any part of His vineyard where He may call me.

With all my heart I love this work, those who lead it, and those who strive to live its teachings. I hope and pray that I shall always be numbered with the faithful Latter-day Saints.

Have been at my desk in the bedroom-office most of the day. Had conferences with air and boat transportation officials. Received and answered much correspondence and sent a bulletin to mission presidents together with a proposed itinerary for the visit of President Sonne and myself to the ten missions. (ETB Journal.)

We enjoyed a most spiritual conference. We all missed my husband so much. (FAB Journal.)

SUNDAY, OCTOBER 6, 1946:
LONDON AND BIRMINGHAM, ENGLAND

Left London by car for Birmingham. The ride through the beautiful green countryside of ole England is a delight to behold — green fields verdant with forage, lovely fall flowers in profusion, wooded lanes bordered with soft green and lined with stately trees, and old ivy-covered rock walls or hawthorne hedges. Peaceful Ayreshire and Shorthorn cattle, Shire and Clydesdale horses, and Cotswold and black-faced sheep rested or grazed leisurely in the fertile pastures as we sped through one picturesque village after another for three-and-one-half hours. It was a most soul-satisfying experience gripping me almost to complete silence. In every direction were views to challenge and invite the brush of the landscape artist.

We were greeted warmly by the Saints who had assembled at the Conway Road School in Sparkbrook, Birmingham. There we enjoyed three glorious sessions of conference interspersed with pleasant visits, conferences with small groups and individuals. I signed programs and autographed books until I emptied two fountain pens and got writer's cramp—and still they kept coming.

The Lord poured out his Spirit in rich abundance on the more than 600 who attended. Three representatives of the press were present and interviewed me. They became so interested in the morning session they returned in the evening, unknown to me.

The spirit in this mission has greatly improved and the outlook is bright. (ETB Journal.)

In contemplation of returning to the United States in the near future, I bade farewell to the British Saints and expressed my regret that it will be necessary to leave the work among the Saints of Europe in which I am now engaged. I then recalled prophecies concerning events which will occur in the last days—the return of the Jews to Palestine and the part Great Britain is to play in this great movement. However, I warned that all is not well with the British nation, that there is much sin and a great need for national repentance in order to escape the pending judgments promised those who forsake God. I urged greater love of liberty and freedom and independence by the British people. (European Mission History.)

MONDAY, OCTOBER 7, 1946:
LONDON AND BIRMINGHAM, ENGLAND

We held a glorious meeting with the fifty missionaries of this mission. There was an inspiring spirit present and everyone was evidently touched to the heart. This is a strong group of missionaries and their spirit is excellent.

God bless them as they bring the much-needed message of the restored gospel to this great people.

Drove home to London, arriving at 7:00 P.M. with three missionaries coming with us. After an hour of hymn singing around the piano in our living room, I read through most of my accumulation of mail including sweet and comforting words from my ever-devoted wife. Retired at 10:15. (ETB Journal.)

TUESDAY, OCTOBER 8, 1946:
LONDON, ENGLAND, AND AMSTERDAM, NETHERLANDS

Office dictating then to KLM (Dutch Airlines) office and on to Amsterdam where I was met by President Zappey of the Netherlands Mission.

We then left by Citroen car to drive part way to Gronigen in northern Netherlands. All went well until we arrived at the west end of the dike across an arm of the North Sea at Den Dover. Here President Zappey became very sick. After stopping several times, he was riding quite comfortably when the motor became very hot and began to ping. After some wait in the cold on the dike twelve miles from the mainland with the North Sea rolling in on either side, some men in a car pulled us in to Holinger.

After considerable effort and delay, we found a doctor and a rooming house. After making Brother Zappey comfortable and invoking the blessings of the Lord upon him through administration, in which I anointed him and sealed the anointing, I retired at 1:30 A.M. (ETB Journal.)

WEDNESDAY, OCTOBER 9, 1946:
GRONINGEN, NETHERLANDS

Rose and got a mechanic and found all radiator water had been lost through a faulty connection yesterday morning at a garage. Fixed it up promptly and after the doctor checked Brother Zappey, who is much better, we set out for Groningen.

After inspecting several building sites, we took an option on 900 square meters in a lovely new area overlooking an artificial lake in a park.

Left for Utrecht via Assen, Meppel, and Zwolle. (ETB Journal.)

SATURDAY, OCTOBER 12, 1946:
LONDON, ENGLAND

This has been a busy and most happy day, as have all the days of the past eight-and-a-half months in Europe. Possibly at no time since arriving in Europe have I felt so "caught up" with my work as tonight. Practically all correspondence is taken care of, problems answered, material of a current nature read, and filing done. If I can complete a call tonight to Sweden that has been pending all day, the day will be complete and I can leave for Manchester in the morning with no worries or pressing problems on my mind as I attend the district conference and go on to Liverpool to consider the sale and possible purchase of properties for that branch.

Have completed tentative plans for the visit of President Sonne and myself to the mission beginning November 2. I pray that all will work out satisfactorily under the blessings of the Lord. (ETB Journal.)

MONDAY, OCTOBER 14, 1946:
ROCHDALE, LIVERPOOL, AND LONDON, ENGLAND

Left Rochdale for Liverpool, where we inspected the Liverpool Branch property which is in a deplorable condition and a discredit to the Church. I made recommendations for repairs, renovations, and general clean up based on a plan to be prepared by a competent architect.

Drove to London via the beautiful tunnel under the Mercy River, Chester, etc. (ETB Journal.)

Saw doctor and he said I was overworking. He said I should have an operation as soon as possible.

201

My husband and I knew before he left for Europe that I was to have an operation. The operation has been brought on because of conditions developing from giving birth to the most lovely and perfect children.

I know that the Lord will bless me in my operation that I will be stronger and feel better physically than I ever have in my life. Whatever the Lord wishes for me to have I know will be right.

I have been very close to my children. I feel it is a mother's duty and responsibility to stay home and teach and train her children as they should be taught and keep them well and strong, both spiritually and physically.

Naturally at times I have longed to go out with my husband on trips that he goes on, but then I say, "No, I should not go and leave my children for someone else to take care of. It is my place as a mother to be with them until they are married. If we go on a trip, we as a family will all go together. I can take these trips with my husband when my children are married and on their own. But they need me now, and I have a double responsibility to take the place of both mother and father.

I am going to see that I do all within my power and strength to see that our children have the proper training, home life, and love, and they need me to stay home with them more than ever because of their father having to be away so much.

If more mothers would stay home more with their children and pal and play and talk and advise and counsel with them, there would be few problems with our girls and boys or with juvenile delinquency.

Parents would receive big dividends if they stayed close and at home with their children and not out to parties and traveling so much. (FAB Journal.)

WEDNESDAY, OCTOBER 16, 1946:
LONDON, ENGLAND

Office dictating answers to correspondence, telephoning, and an hour's conference with Mr. Vivian Meik from the editorial staff of *The People*. Mr. Meik, who is most friendly toward the Church and who, through the efforts of the Genealogical Society, has learned that some of his relatives are members of the Church, spoke in highest terms of our people. *The People* paper has the largest circulation of any paper in the English language, five-and-one-half million. He said, among other things, that our people seemed to be the only ones who were satisfied in their hearts and who had no fear for the future. He asked for literature, which was provided, and for further conferences.

Visited the world-famous Madame Tussaud's wax works exhibition and then returned to my quarters and wrote and signed letters. (ETB Journal.)

I think it best until you return that the General Authorities are not aware or concerned or told of my condition, because I have always wanted you to stay in the mission as long as it is necessary for you to do the work of the Lord, as it should be done, no matter what may come or develop with me and our children. I can carry on satisfactorily and I know all will be well. I don't want the Church Authorities to be concerned about me. They have a heavy enough load to carry without added concern.

I am so thankful I have been able to hold up and carry through in doing my small part of your mission at home so you could go to Europe and do such a marvelous work for thousands of distressed people and for you to be able to stay the full time that the General Authorities desired that you did, and the Lord would bless me so the operation wouldn't have to be done until you filled your mission completely. The Lord has surely blessed my humble efforts and helped me on so very much. Please don't worry about me. The Lord won't fail me.

The added responsibilities that have been mine the past year, with your having been in Europe, have no doubt been the main factors in bringing on this added condition in my body. But I am thankful to the Lord for all of it, and I know and feel that the Lord was indeed overly good to me in blessing me and our home with the choice little spirit and body of our dear little Flora Beth and preserving my life. I would go through it all again, and more if it were necessary, to have more of God's choice spirits. But I suppose now the Lord feels we have done all within our part and power and we have our share, and I am indeed thankful for them and grateful beyond words to express thanks for our choice six children — and they are indeed choice.

Too, the Lord gave me such added strength and blessings during Flora Beth's illness. His blessings were showered down upon both of us — so that it didn't interfere in your spirit and work to be able to carry on with your great task as president of the European Mission. I am so grateful and thankful to the Lord for His abundant blessings that He has and is showering down upon me so constantly. I feel at times I don't deserve them all. I hope and pray I shall always be worthy of His many blessings.

I am so desirous at all times to please you and the Lord and to make you most happy — to always help you and the Church my utmost in furthering the Lord's work upon the earth. At times since you have been gone, when the load seemed to get a bit heavy, I would be all the more determined to try and work harder, to pray harder and ask the Lord to help me always put on a better "front" and to help me carry on with a cheerful happy influence of gratitude for the bigger and finer things in life and the life to come.

I have ever felt that you and our family and I were indeed very privileged to be chosen and selected to carry through with such a call as we have been given. I have felt and I know that we would be given added blessings, both in this life and the life to come, if we did our part. I know that both you and I, our family, and thousands of other people in Europe and elsewhere have already witnessed and enjoyed many added blessings because of this call that has come to you and our family. It has brought a deeper, diviner, and purer love for us both toward each other and our family. Our testimonies have been greatly increased and countless other blessings have opened up and been brought to us. (FAB to ETB.)

SUNDAY, OCTOBER 20, 1946:
BERLIN, GERMANY

The second shipment of Church welfare supplies, consisting of thirty-five tons of food products, has just arrived in Berlin. The first shipment, received about a month ago, is stored in the mission home, from which point it is being distributed throughout the various districts according to need. The clothing is being carefully sorted and will be a great blessing to the Saints of the mission as it reaches them at the beginning of the winter season.

I wish you could have seen the clothes as they had them neatly arranged on the floors and in cabinets at the mission home and witnessed the expressions of gratitude, both facial and by word of mouth, from the mission presidency and other Saints. The brethren of the presidency were already wearing some of the items of clothing, the first they have been able to obtain in many years. They are, no doubt, as well, if not better, dressed than any Germans in Berlin today. (European Mission History.)

TUESDAY, OCTOBER 22, 1946:
BERLIN AND FRANKFURT, GERMANY

Arrived in Berlin and were required to wait on account of "low ceiling" before taking off for Frankfurt. On arrival there we learned that the two planes for London had left and we would have to wait until morning. (ETB Journal.)

WEDNESDAY, OCTOBER 23, 1946:
FRANKFURT, GERMANY

Left for the airport hoping to get an early plane to London. One postponement after another on account of bad weather at Frankfurt and London caused us to spend the entire day at the airport. I remained in Frankfurt hoping weather would permit me to leave in the morning by plane. (ETB Journal.)

Thursday, October 24, 1946:
Frankfurt, Germany, and London, England

Weather is clear. Went to airport, left for London. Rode to London with an official of the U.S. State Department and was at my desk to find it piled high with mail, including four letters from my faithful wife.

The letters from my wife brought the sad news that Flora will have to submit to an operation of major character, largely due to overwork and excessive strain. There was some evidence of this before I left home. In fact, we had spoken to the doctor about it only a few days before my call came from the First Presidency to leave on this mission "as soon as possible." We, of course, postponed the operation and I left in a few days.

Now the doctor says the operation should be taken care of promptly. Flora is so sweet and brave about it all and assures me that our planned vacation and rest period, which will now have to be foregone, is perfectly all right and that she is perfectly contented and happy.

I am advising her to seek a blessing at the hands of the brethren and then meet me in New York from which point we will go directly home and then consider the operation question. She has worked so hard and ceaselessly and has been so brave and uncomplaining all during my absence. I am truly grateful for her sterling character. She is without doubt one of the chosen daughters of our Heavenly Father and a choice daughter of Zion. God bless her. May I be worthy of her eternal companionship. (ETB Journal.)

Friday, October 25, 1946:
London, England

Dictating all day. No further word from home and no word from President Sonne, who is delayed in New York City because of the vicious and prolonged maritime strike. (ETB Journal.)

Saturday, October 26, 1946:
London, England

Received an early (3:00 A.M.) call that my wife was trying to reach me. After an hour's wait the word came that the call was cancelled. After considerable anxiety I placed a call for her at 5:00 A.M. The call was not completed until 9:00 P.M., and then the connection was poor so we could not be fully understood.

I gleaned, however, that Flora, Dr. Skidmore, et al. feel the operation should take place early in November and that she requests that I say nothing to the General Authorities about it because she doesn't want my mission to be affected in any way.

I explained I'd likely be coming home in early December, but she feels it should not be postponed but that all will be well and the Lord will be with her. We could hardly talk for crying, but her last words were, "Don't tell the Brethren but stay and fill your mission."

After an hour of prayer and meditation I wrote her an airmail special delivery letter making certain suggestions and asking for further information, although Flora said she had written me in detail, which letter has not yet arrived. (ETB Journal.)

Even now some of our Saints have their precious eyesight imperiled, according to reports of physicians, because of the absence of fat in the diet. As Americans, we often find ourselves wishing that our impoverished Saints in these war-torn countries could have even a portion of the excess fat consumed and wasted in the average American home even during this period of short supply. One of the members of the acting mission presidency in Berlin has practically lost the use of his eyes because of a fat deficiency in his diet. We were happy to be able to give him a small can of fat on our visit to Berlin last week, received from a German friend here in London.

Our Saints need practically everything needed to sustain life and health, to say nothing of the many common household supplies that are almost nonexistent in the occupied areas today. However, the greatest need is for fat and sugar. (European Mission History.)

SUNDAY, OCTOBER 27, 194:
LONDON, ENGLAND

This has been a day of fasting, prayer, and meditation which I have greatly appreciated. I have been blessed with the assurance from my Heavenly Father that all is well and that Flora will be all right whether the operation is performed now in my absence or later on my return. I am so anxious that one of the Brethren administer to her before any operation is performed and that as the decision is made to operate, if this seems best, that the Brethren be apprised of it so that they can join their faith with ours in Flora's behalf. This can be done just prior to the operation so that there will be no feeling of obligation to call me home before my mission is completed.

There is so much to be done yet to get President Sonne acquainted with conditions here and complete plans already projected pertaining to welfare distribution, missionary work, etc. And yet I long to be close to Flora if she is to go through this serious ordeal. She is so brave, faithful, and unselfish. She has never had any thought of fear for herself, and complete unselfishness has always characterized her attitude when she is involved. She exercises such extreme care for others and so little for herself. (ETB Journal.)

MONDAY, OCTOBER 28, 1946:
LONDON, ENGLAND

It is nine months today since I was set apart by the First Presidency for this mission. Throughout the entire period the Lord has been near me. Never once have I been downhearted or discouraged. Not one murmur has come

208

from my wife or children. To them it has been "our mission," and they have been true blue.

My heart fills with deep gratitude as I contemplate all my blessings. Received a letter from Flora, in fact the original and a copy, the latter sent in care of the British Mission, telling that her condition is such that she and the doctor feel an operation is necessary without undue delay. After prayerful consideration I cabled her as follows: "Just received your sweet brave letters regarding operation. Sonne still in New York. Can't complete mission and return before December sixth. Placing confidential call to Brother Lee requesting he see you and doctor and airmail me. Must do what's best for your health immediately. The Lord will safeguard you. God bless you, darling. Affectionately, T."

After sending cable, I talked to Brother Lee at his home and explained Flora's condition and doctor's advice. He agreed to follow through and write me. We both could hardly speak because of emotion. I have prayed much about the matter and feel some better about the operation in my absence, although naturally during this serious period I'd like to be close to home. (ETB Journal.)

I received a wonderful cable from my husband asking the Lord to bless me and do all I should to take proper care of myself.

Elder Harold B. Lee and his good wife called on me this evening. My darling husband had talked by telephone from London to Brother Lee about my physical condition. Brother Lee told me that my husband said over the phone that there were three things he wanted Brother Lee to do. First, see our doctor; second, call and see me; third, give his sweetheart a blessing.

Brother Lee gave me a most glorious and comforting blessing. My husband wanted so much to be at my side and be with me when I was to have my operation. After the blessing Elder Lee gave me, I felt impressed it would be safe and all right if I waited until my husband came home.

My doctor and Elder Lee said I must get help in the home and be off my feet as much as possible if I were going to postpone my operation. I have a good girl come once a week and clean now, and I have refused and turned down all invitations to parties. I have been invited out so many places but feel my health is more important and taking care of our family. So what strength I have I give it to my home and family and writing my wonderful husband. (FAB Journal.)

TUESDAY, OCTOBER 29, 1946:
LONDON, ENGLAND

Office all day dictating and reading mail and in conferences. Wrote Flora, as I plan to do each day until I'm with her, and received a letter from her in a rather sad and somewhat lonely tone which concerns me greatly. I can well imagine she is worried and not well and, as a result, her usually cheerful optimistic spirit is bound to be affected. How I wish I could be close to her. Yet I know that the Lord will overrule all things for our good and that He will speak peace to our souls and preserve her during this crisis. May God grant it may be so. (ETB Journal.)

THURSDAY, OCTOBER 31, 1946:
LONDON, ENGLAND

Another day at my desk. (ETB Journal.)

Conditions today, generally speaking, in the war-torn countries of Europe are much worse than any conditions which have existed here within the memory of any of the brethren who are coming here as missionaries. Although there has been considerable improvement during the past year, the situation still remains very grim. Food is very, very short in quantity, relatively poor in quality, and limited in variety. The fuel situation is very serious throughout all of Europe both in the war-torn countries and those which were not actively engaged in war. Last winter was a mild winter in Europe. We don't know what this winter will be, but October has been the coldest October in five years and the prospects are not encouraging. The housing situation continues to be most acute. (European Mission History.)

FRIDAY, NOVEMBER 1, 1946:
LONDON, ENGLAND

At the office all day. Also prepared a short article for the *Children's Friend*. (ETB Journal.)

SATURDAY, NOVEMBER 2, 1946:
UTRECHT, NETHERLANDS

My heart was filled with joy to receive an encouraging letter from my wife telling me the doctor had approved postponement of her operation until after my return, providing she gets help in the home and doesn't overdo.

She told of Brother Harold B. Lee coming to the home at my telephone request and giving her a lovely blessing, promising that the operation would be successful and she would recover — that her mission was not finished, but that she would live long and enjoy even richer blessings in the future than she has in her past life. It is all most encouraging to both of us.

We left for Amsterdam in an army DC-3 with BOAC seats. The ceiling was somewhat low, but above the clouds and fog it was quite satisfactory although dark on these short days of late autumn. We arrived safely in Amsterdam two hours later and were met by President Zappey, who drove us to Utrecht where we attended the latter part of a missionwide MIA program with some 800 in attendance.

Retired in a small dirty, cold room — the only space available according to the district president. Undressed in the dark because there were no shades. Slept very little but had more comfort than in some places in Europe, particularly Germany. (ETB Journal.)

Hundreds of people chartered private buses, others came by rail and bicycle to join in this great occasion — the

211

largest group ever assembled at a missionwide conference in Holland.

It was interesting to note that, through the efficiently organized Church welfare program of this mission, the Saints are looking very healthy and warmly dressed. Many of those in attendance were proudly wearing American welfare clothing. All of the timely aid received from Zion has strengthened the bonds of love and brotherhood, and the members were happy to be able to express their gratitude and appreciation.

Songs, skits, and group demonstrations under the direction of the MIA made for a most happy entertainment. People were loath to leave for their various overnight quarters and remained nearly two hours after the program ended, chatting with each other, shaking hands, and trying to catch up on a year's visiting in the short time available to do so. (European Mission History.)

SUNDAY, NOVEMBER 3, 1946:
UTRECHT, NETHERLANDS

Spent a glorious and full day in a missionwide conference held in a large public hall in Utrecht. More than 1,000 Saints and friends from the five districts were present, and the Lord poured out his Spirit richly. The Saints were so happy and kind and so delighted to be together that it was more than two-and-a-half hours after the meeting closed before we could get away.

A feature of the conference was a singing mothers chorus and a combined chorus of about 300 voices, all of which was recorded and played back after the meeting in part. The singing mothers were clothed largely in welfare clothes, but there were not enough white blouses for all and some didn't fit very well. Most of the Saints were wearing clothes from Zion. (ETB Journal.)

This month I have turned down many lovely invitations and parties that many kind friends have invited me to because of my

212

physical condition. The doctor says I must be careful. If I do my housework and care for the children properly, that takes the time up fully.

Everyone has been so kind, good, and thoughtful during my husband's absence, and all my life I have been so greatly blessed, and I hope and pray I shall always live to merit and deserve such blessings. (FAB Journal.)

MONDAY, NOVEMBER 4, 1946:
UTRECHT AND AMSTERDAM, NETHERLANDS; LONDON, ENGLAND

After further conferences with President Zappey and mission staff, we were driven to Amsterdam where we caught the plane to London and arrived at the office one hour later.

Read mail for an hour. I am so anxious to reach home as soon as possible for Flora's sake, so she can complete her hospitalization before Christmas if possible. (ETB Journal.)

FRIDAY, NOVEMBER 8, 1946:
LONDON, ENGLAND; GOTEBORG AND STOCKHOLM, SWEDEN

Office until noon. Left for Stockholm; delayed forty-five minutes for weather clearance. Stopped at Goteborg two-and-one-half hours later after experiencing the setting of the sun and the rising of the moon through the fluffy clouds as we sped at 175 miles per hour above them at an elevation above ground of 6,500 feet.

At Goteborg the passport control officers, to my embarrassment, told me my passport visa expired November 1. However, after negotiations extending during our entire stop of forty-five minutes, during which I missed my dinner, they approved my journey and issued an emergency permit.

Arrived in Stockholm and was met by mission authorities. (ETB Journal.)

213

SUNDAY, NOVEMBER 10, 1946:
GAVLE, ESKILSTUNA, AND STOCKHOLM, SWEDEN

Left Gavle by car for Eskilstuna. After losing our way and having some car trouble, we arrived one-and-a-half hours late for meeting to find the people still waiting.

After a lovely meeting and interviews with two newspaper reporters, we took refreshments with the Saints.

We left for Stockholm. Held a large public meeting at which I spoke on the Word of Wisdom. Later I addressed and visited with the fireside group of fifty fine young people.

After telephone calls and cables to the First Presidency and the Danish Mission, I retired at 12 midnight. (ETB Journal.)

MONDAY, NOVEMBER 11, 1946:
STOCKHOLM, SWEDEN; COPENHAGEN, DENMARK; LONDON, ENGLAND

Arose and wrote letters to my family and reported at the Swedish Mission home. Left for Copenhagen and spent three pleasant hours with President Alma L. Petersen of the Danish Mission and flew on to London, arriving to find all well and much mail, including two sweet letters from my ever-faithful wife. (ETB Journal.)

WEDNESDAY, NOVEMBER 13, 1946:
LONDON, ENGLAND

Office all day. Packed trunk for boat freight shipment to Salt Lake City. (ETB Journal.)

FRIDAY, NOVEMBER 15, 1946:
LONDON, ENGLAND

Arose and made plans for discussions with Presidents Sonne and Stover at Southampton and further with Sonne in London. Arranged for President Barker to meet the *S.S. Washington* at Le Havre tomorrow. Also completed reser-

President Benson greets President and Sister Alma Sonne upon their arrival in England.

vations and other plans for our continental tour. Dictated about half the day. (ETB Journal.)

SATURDAY, NOVEMBER 16, 1946:
LONDON AND SOUTHAMPTON, ENGLAND

Left for Southampton where I met the *S.S. Washington*. After greeting President and Sister Sonne, I went aboard and gave instructions to President Walter Stover for Berlin and the missionaries for Switzerland and France. Were successful in clearing customs without being charged duty and returned to London.

Lunched with Sonnes in our rooms. Then I introduced them to our humble flat and the temporary accommodations for them during our visit on the Continent and long-time possibilities for quarters for the future.

It is good to have them here, and I hope I can get President Sonne fully acquainted with conditions in the missions so I can leave with the assurance I've done all I can to help him get started on his new responsibilities. (ETB Journal.)

SUNDAY, NOVEMBER 17, 1946:
LONDON, ENGLAND

With President Sonne, we held a conference with President Selvoy J. Boyer, the district presidents, and a general meeting as part of the London District conference.

Spent the afternoon and evening going over mission matters with President Sonne, who seemed astonished at the humble accomplishments of the past nine-and-a-half months. Truly as I, of necessity, reviewed them with President Sonne, even I was amazed at the manner in which the Lord has opened the way before us in this glorious mission. (ETB Journal.)

MONDAY, NOVEMBER 18, 1946:
LONDON, ENGLAND

This has been a day of conferences interspersed with dictation and long distance calls. With President Sonne, we had profitable and pleasant conferences.

Retired after rereading the sweetest, loveliest, most faith-promoting and soul-satisfying letter which a man could ever hope to receive from his wife — and this in spite of the fact she is not well. How I love and adore and cherish my darling wife, sweetheart, and companion, Flora. No man ever had a truer, choicer helpmeet. I thank the Lord daily for her and ever pray He will preserve her in health for many years to come and help me to be worthy of her. (ETB Journal.)

TUESDAY, NOVEMBER 19, 1946:
LONDON, ENGLAND; AMSTERDAM, ROTTERDAM, AND
THE HAGUE, NETHERLANDS

Left London with President Sonne for our visit to the nine missions of the Continent and arrived in Amsterdam. Were met by President and Sister Zappey and drove to Rotterdam where we inspected the welfare supplies and warehouse. Then drove to mission headquarters in The Hague. Attended and spoke for an hour through an interpreter and shook hands thereafter with the entire audience of 500—some of them more than once. There was a lovely spirit, and I was deeply moved by their loving good-bye.

The Dutch look so much better than when I first met with them several months ago. They seem better fed and clothed and their spirit is much improved. They are most happy with the fifty missionaries—eleven having arrived the last two weeks. (ETB Journal.)

WEDNESDAY, NOVEMBER 20, 1946:
THE HAGUE, HAARLEM, AND AMSTERDAM, NETHER-
LANDS

After a good night's rest at mission headquarters, we held a conference for one-and-a-half hours with President Zappey and then drove to Haarlem where I inspected a proposed building for purchase. It was found to be unsuitable. Attended a missionary meeting for four hours.

In the evening attended a meeting in the Amsterdam Branch with 300 in attendance. There was a glorious spirit present, and the love of the Saints was most touching as I shook hands with each one after a meeting in which many tears were shed.

Several gifts were presented, including a lovely silver set from President and Sister Zappey, a famous cake packed for shipping from the Groningen Branch, and some beautiful Dutch needlework from the Amsterdam Branch. (ETB Journal.)

217

THURSDAY, NOVEMBER 21, 1946:
AMSTERDAM, NETHERLANDS, AND COPENHAGEN,
DENMARK

Arose and drove to the airport, where I bade a fond farewell to President and Sister Zappey.

Arrived at Copenhagen. President Alma L. Petersen met us and we went to the mission home.

After a short visit and lovely dinner, we held a meeting with President Petersen, rested a bit, and then held a most inspiring meeting with Saints and friends. It was a meeting I shall long remember — filled with the Spirit and with so much love and harmony. Many tears were shed from the time the congregation stood as we entered until we sang "God Be with You" and shook the hands of each one and lingered long to visit.

Never have I felt my feelings more tender and had my heart go out to a people more than here. How I would like to return with my good Danish-Scottish wife to the land of her father. (ETB Journal.)

MONDAY, NOVEMBER 25, 1946:
STOCKHOLM, SWEDEN

As we pulled in to Stockholm station, the strains of "God Bless America" entered the door of our sleeping car. The Blomquist family, missionaries, and some fifty Saints had come to welcome us to the Swedish Mission.

Then followed interviews and photos with the press, a meeting with the fifty missionaries, inspection of buildings, radio broadcast, and public meeting at night interspersed with important conferences with President Eben R.T. Blomquist regarding building purchases and other problems.

It was hard to leave the Saints here. Their love is so deep and sincere. We lingered in fond good-byes for over two hours after the meeting ended. Then I signed some 100 booklets containing my "Farewell! God Bless You" message with a cut of my family on the front and a lovely letter from President Blomquist on behalf of all the Saints. This has ended another day long to be remembered. (ETB Journal.)

TUESDAY, NOVEMBER 26, 1946:
STOCKHOLM, SWEDEN, AND PRAGUE, CZECHOSLOVAKIA

We left Stockholm by plane for Prague, Czechoslovakia. We were greeted by Saints laden with flowers and went to our hotel and into immediate conference with President Toronto as we ate fruit in my room given us by the Swedish Saints.

We held a public meeting with about 125 in attendance, two-thirds of whom were nonmembers. Little girls in native costumes greeted us and we had a glorious meeting. Afterward we administered to the Saints and visited with them for two hours.

It was hard to say good-bye. Some had come great distances at considerable sacrifice.

Returning to the hotel, we held conference further with President Toronto until midnight. The Saints in Brno with whom I held a meeting last summer presented me with a lovely handmade silk tablecloth. (ETB Journal.)

President George Albert Smith called me by telephone to wish us a pleasant Thanksgiving and see how we all were. (FAB Journal.)

THURSDAY, NOVEMBER 28, 1946:
BASEL, SWITZERLAND

Thanksgiving Day. Meeting with missionaries, a Thanksgiving dinner at the Basel chapel with the missionaries, and a splendid meeting with Saints and friends made a busy and pleasant day. (ETB Journal.)

The boys went to the football game and when they came home, they insisted the girls and I go to a movie show. We went and enjoyed it. It was very good. The name of it was "I've Always Loved You." It made me think of my devoted and loving husband because I have always loved and admired him to the fullest — from the first day I met and knew him.

We surely missed having with us my wonderful husband and father to our children on this Thanksgiving day. (FAB Journal.)

SUNDAY, DECEMBER 1, 1946:
PARIS, FRANCE

This has been a busy, happy day. Met with President Barker in the early morning, missionaries and district presidents, and with Saints and friends. All meetings were held in the lovely mission home. I also conferred with representatives of the Paris press.

Boarded the train for Frankfurt (entirely military) and bade President Barker farewell. (ETB Journal.)

Today was fast Sunday. I went to church with the six children. I bore my testimony in fast meeting. I felt I should express my gratitude to the Lord and the ward members for the many blessings I have been blessed with and for the love and kindness that the Yale Ward members have shown to me. I also expressed my great appreciation for my wonderful husband and for our precious family.

I said how we sisters should encourage our husbands and male members to do their duty in the Church and the Lord would bless us greatly for the same. I said I was proud of the work my husband was doing and had done as president of the European Mission. I said it is natural for us to have our lonely moments when our husbands are called to perform duties in the Church (that is natural when we love them dearly), but I said the Lord will bless us and there are compensations and added blessings that the Lord will make up to us threefold if we place our church work first and always do our duty in the Church. Above all, we will have blessings rich and everlasting in this world and eternally forever and ever. Our families will be better and greater joys will be ours. (FAB Journal.)

MONDAY, DECEMBER 2, 1946:
FRANKFURT, GERMANY

Arrived in Frankfurt with the trainload of army and U.S. military government personnel and began meetings, which occupied the entire day, with President Max Zimmer, district presidents, and mission auxiliary heads and a public meeting with the Saints.

I shall never forget this meeting with these poor Saints and their loving farewell. Tears filled their eyes as I spoke to them, and I had difficulty speaking because of the emotion which welled up in my bosom. President Zimmer was most kind in his comments.

The Saints sang as the closing song their farewell song as we all wept tears of love and gratitude. Then I stood at the door and shook hands with each of the 300 to 400 present as my hand and arm, already sore from previous experiences, ached. But I could not refrain from responding to the wishes of these poor but happy and great souls who have such great love for the gospel and the leaders of the Church.

There isn't anything that is right I wouldn't do for them. How I wish I had the power to lift them from their distress and suffering. Gladly would I give every material thing in life to ease their discomfort and pain. God bless them and keep them true to the faith and bring us together again where starvation, cold, and suffering are no more. (ETB Journal.)

TUESDAY, DECEMBER 3, 1946:
FRANKFURT, GERMANY

Arose at 4:30 A.M. Couldn't sleep because of thoughts of the many problems facing us in Germany, pointed out as they were at our district presidents' conference yesterday.

With President Alma Sonne, went to USFET head-quarters to present Brother Sonne to some of my acquaintances and confer with military officials. Had a most pleasant conference with Commanding General Joseph T. McNarney and several others.

Met with President Max Zimmer and Brother Sorenson, a major of the welfare department of USFET.

Later we drove out to Langen and visited our refugees housed there, some in Swiss army barracks we were able to purchase in Switzerland. The condition of these Saints is much improved since I last visited them — thanks to welfare supplies, purchases made in Switzerland, and the industry of the people.

Met further with President Zimmer and took the overnight train ("Berliner") for Berlin, bidding President Zimmer a fond farewell. We have traveled much together in the past ten months in Germany, sleeping, eating, working, weeping, and praying together. He is a magnanimous soul with a great love for the German people of which he is one although living in Switzerland for many years. (ETB Journal.)

President George Albert Smith called on the telephone to see how I and the family are getting along. He said he was writing my husband and wanted to tell him all was well with us. (FAB Journal.)

WEDNESDAY, DECEMBER 4, 1946:
BERLIN, GERMANY

Arrived in Berlin and were met by President Walter Stover, Francis Gasser, and Sister Eugene Merrill. We went to the lovely Merrill home where we held a brief meeting and then went to OMGUS headquarters, registered with the Visitors Bureau, secured return transportation, conferred with Director of Office of Political Affairs, called at the offices of General Lucius D. Clay, Deputy Military

Governor, Robert D. Murphy, Ambassador and U.S. Political Adviser for U.S., et al.

We met with a packed hall of 774 Saints from the Berlin District in an inspirational meeting. I released the acting mission presidency, consisting of Richard Ranglack, Paul Langheinrich, and Max Jeske, and the Saints voted a hearty vote of appreciation and enthusiastically sustained President Walter Stover.

With tear-dimmed eyes I bade a loving farewell to these devoted Saints whose conditions have improved greatly since I first met them in early March, as many of them lingered for more than an hour to shake hands, some two or three times, and expressed to me their love and blessing. I shall never forget them.

One of the most touching things was the presentation to me of a lovely hand-embroidered book cover from our refugees at Wolfsgruen.

We held a meeting with President Stover and the retiring presidency and met with the U.S. servicemen and military government LDS group. Retired at midnight. (ETB Journal.)

THURSDAY, DECEMBER 5, 1946:
BERLIN, GERMANY

Arose and after an hour's work in my room and breakfast, we went to the mission home for a meeting with local missionaries (twenty-seven) and district presidents for three hours. Held conferences with Dr. C. Arild Olsen, Dr. Kazenurg Libera of the Polish Military Mission, et al.

In the evening with Brother and Sister Eugene H. Merrill were dinner guests at Dr. and Mrs. Olsen's. After the dinner some twenty people came in, including President Walter Stover, Richard Ranglack, our Berlin District president, Brother Schultze, and Brother Francis Gasser of our Church, and representatives of several churches, some of whom were attached to Dr. Olsen's Religious Affairs Branch of OMGUS. Represented were Lutherans, Mennonites, Episcopalians, Methodists, Catholics, Quakers, and others.

Then, according to previous invitation, President Sonne and I for two hours told the attentive and interested group about the Church — its doctrines, organization, work in Europe, and distinctive features such as welfare work, tithing, temple work, and our missionary system. Under the blessings of the Lord it was well received.

Later in a brief personal conversation I told Dr. Olsen the story of the Restoration and the Prophet Joseph. He was not only interested, but expressed regret he had not asked us to relate this great event. We did not do so because he had asked for other things. However, Dr. Olsen invited representatives of the Church to come for another evening to meet with the group to present the account of the Restoration. I was able to arrange for our East German Mission authorities to give a series of lectures before several large groups in Berlin. Truly the Lord blessed us, and I pray that fruitful seeds were sown.

The joy of our group was increased when, as I was leaving, Dr. Olsen informed me that President Stover's request for an extension of his military permit had been approved. He also said that OMGUS, through his office, would approve his remaining in Germany for an indefinite period if the Russians would approve entrance into the Russian Zone, which I feel can be accomplished because the Lord wants him to stay. (ETB Journal.)

Today I sent the last letter to Europe that would reach my husband before he arrives home to us again. We can hardly wait. We are so happy and so very thrilled about his arrival.

We are indeed happy that he was able to complete his mission fully and so exceptionally well and stay as long as he was called to do. We rejoice greatly for the wonderful work and mission he has done and that we can enjoy his sweet presence and self again. (FAB Journal.)

FRIDAY, DECEMBER 6, 1946:
BERLIN AND FRANKFURT, GERMANY

Arose and wrote up diary and notes and a short letter to my devoted wife. Then began our conferences at the mission home, with International Red Cross officials, and with Mr. Bevier, head of the welfare work of OMGUS and two of our LDS boys with that department.

Plans were completed for the future distribution of our supplies to our members through the German Central Committee at Stuttgart for the U.S., British, and French Zones and the two German committees in Berlin for the Berlin area and the Russian Zone.

After conferences with President Walter Stover, he took us to the train for Frankfurt. President Sonne and I gave further attention to future plans as we rode toward Frankfurt. President Sonne seems well pleased with conditions found in the missions, the unusual cooperation which I have been able, with the blessings of the Lord, to establish with military authorities, and is high in his praise of my humble "pioneering work, " as he calls it. (ETB Journal.)

SATURDAY, DECEMBER 7, 1946:
FRANKFURT, GERMANY, AND AMSTERDAM, NETHER-
LANDS

Arrived in Frankfurt and were met by President Max Zimmer, who drove us quickly to the airport. After waiting a bit, the flight was cancelled until tomorrow.

As we left for our car, acting on an impression, I checked with officials of American Overseas Airways (just opening offices here) and after some persuasion was given two seats to Amsterdam with the promise they'd wire for earliest space to London. The time intervening was spent in conference with President Zimmer and at the airport, where I had a most pleasant visit with my former acquaintance, Senator Lodge of Massachusetts, who rode on the same plane (DC-4 Skymaster) to Amsterdam.

On arrival we learned the earliest space was Monday, December 9. After hurried phoning, holding of KLM bus, etc., we booked passage on a Channel boat from the Hook of Holland to Harwich. (ETB Journal.)

SUNDAY, DECEMBER 8, 1946:
LONDON, ENGLAND

Had a pleasant voyage. Arose at 4:30 A.M. and enjoyed a half hour on deck in the clear night with a full moon and a refreshing breeze. Then I did some writing before we docked.

Drove to London where I began to read and answer a large accumulation of mail, including letters from my family.

I attended and spoke at the sacrament meeting of the London Branch. Later ate supper and conferred with the Sonnes. (ETB Journal.)

MONDAY, DECEMBER 9, 1946:
LONDON, ENGLAND

I'm constantly singing and walking on air in contemplation of our sweet meeting. Time is so short. I'm working almost night and day to complete the work fully. Worked until after eleven last night and started again this morning at five. (ETB to FAB.)

Darling mine, this will be my last letter before I see you. In fact, I may arrive before this unless I'm delayed or this letter makes perfect connections.

Sweetheart, from the bottom of my heart I thank the Lord for you and thank you for your undeviating loyalty and support. Your letters, next to the sustaining power of the Spirit of the Lord, have been most helpful to me during the ten-and-a-half months I've been away from you. Thanks so much, darling, for your constancy, love and encouragement. I love you so very much — more than when I left you, if such a thing is possible.

I shall always cherish you, dear, and bless the day we first met and the day you became mine for all eternity. How I adore you, dearest.

Thanks so much for your last two letters which were handed to me as I arrived in England—also thank the children for their lovely letters.

I have gone over everything with President Sonne and feel I can leave day after tomorrow confident I've done everything possible to help him get started. We've enjoyed the trip together. Will tell you all soon, darling. (ETB to FAB.)

TUESDAY, DECEMBER 10, 1946:
LONDON, ENGLAND

Further office work.

Two distributions of welfare supplies have been made to all districts in the two German missions, and some additional supplies are on hand in Geneva. One carload of cracked wheat is enroute, and today one mixed car of concentrated foods and two cars of cracked wheat were requested of the First Presidency. Some authorization was given for limited contributions of cracked wheat and powdered milk for general relief in the child-feeding program in the four zones and Berlin.

With the arrival of these supplies, a small shipment to Syria, and a little fat to Holland, plus some few purchases of fat and blankets in Switzerland, ample supplies will be available for the next six months plus a backlog for safety. Food packages have already been mailed to scattered Saints through CARE and the regular eleven-pound food packages and some welfare clothing from our stocks in Paris and Prague.

The entire program is working smoothly in Europe now and everywhere the needs of our people for food, clothing and bedding are pretty well taken care of insofar as these necessities are concerned.

The conditions throughout the missions are good and

so much better than ten months ago when I arrived, when there was suffering and distress everywhere, no mission presidents anywhere in continental Europe, and the entire economy of most of the nations was badly broken down.

I can leave Europe now feeling our entire program is on a solid foundation and the conditions of the Saints much improved. Truly the Lord has blessed our efforts. (ETB Journal.)

In a very real sense the history of this eventful mission would be incomplete were deserving tribute not paid to the profound influence exerted upon our successful labors by my devoted wife, who remained at home to care for our six children.

During the ten months of our stay in Europe, she faced many perplexities and hardships. Although her own health and strength were often severely taxed, her faith and steadfastness never wavered. Never at any time did she register the slightest complaint or needless anxiety.

Within about three months after our arrival in Europe, she faced a crucial test during the critical illness of our youngest child, who was stricken with pneumonia. Because of her unswerving faith, I feel sure, the power of the priesthood and the blessings of heaven were made manifest in a marvelous manner. Though our little child lay at death's door, she was restored to us, for which we humbly express our gratitude to the Lord.

In the course of our travels in Europe, we frequently lived on very short rations, which was common throughout this stricken continent. Anxious to help us maintain our health and vigor, Sister Benson kept nutritious packages of food coming to our London office so we might supplement our otherwise meager and uninteresting diet. Often she would include a special treat which made us appreciate the more how richly blessed our own nation has been.

Invariably when we were faced with serious decisions or grave situations, a timely letter of encouragement would arrive which would completely dispel the clouds of anxiety and concern which seemed to weigh so heavily upon us at times.

It is my humble testimony that our choice helpmeets and companions contribute immeasurably to the successful completion of such a mission and deserve grateful recognition. Without them, I am sure, we would fall short of achieving fully what we are able to do with their faith and confidence in us. May the Lord bless them richly for their very real contribution to the success that has attended our efforts! (European Mission History.)

WEDNESDAY, DECEMBER 11, 1946:
LONDON, ENGLAND

Began work at 5:30 A.M. Completed all correspondence, transfer of inventories, finances, records, and mission affairs to President Sonne. Held further conferences with President and Sister Sonne, wrote official letters to General Joseph T. McNarney and the Allied Control Commission, and otherwise completed my work.

President Sonne expressed complete satisfaction and said I had done everything possible to acquaint him with conditions to help him get started and that he is in full agreement with all my policies in the European Mission and the instructions and suggestions made.

I feel happy with the results of the past three-and-one-half weeks together, during which period we have been fully united in all things pertaining to our work in Europe.

As I leave, it is with the assurance I have done everything possible to get him properly started and the work well established in Europe. I can't think of one single thing left undone which should have received my attention. I am so grateful to the Lord for his rich blessings.

Left for the air terminal building at twelve noon, where I had lunch with the Sonnes and Brother Babbel. I then boarded the bus for the Heathrow Airport while they followed in the car. After good-byes, clearance of customs,

President Benson prepares to board the Pan Am aircraft "Constellation" enroute home after spending nearly eleven months in Europe.

passport control, and snapshots at the aircraft, I boarded the Pan American Airways Constellation.

Arrived at Shannon Airport in southern Ireland, where we had dinner and were held because of adverse weather over much of the Atlantic. The reports kept shifting us from Shannon via the Azores, south of the British Islands, then via Gander, Newfoundland, direct. Finally it was decided to fly to New York City via Goose Bay and Labrador, Newfoundland.

Got some sleep in the comfortable reclining chairs. Passed through some heavy storms at about midnight making it rough and requiring the fastening of seat belts. (ETB Journal.)

I am having my hair fixed extra nice so I'll look just right when my darling husband returns. We are counting the hours for our dear husband and father to arrive home. (FAB Journal.)

THURSDAY, DECEMBER 12, 1946:
GOOSE BAY AND LABRADOR, NEWFOUNDLAND; NEW
YORK CITY

Arrived Goose Bay. There was heavy snow at this outpost and the temperature was 14 degrees below zero. The runways were lined with banks of snow shoved from the runways by big snowplows. Only one boat per year comes in here, I was told, and that in late July. There are no trains. Gander, Newfoundland, airport is ordinarily used instead of Goose Bay, when weather permits, for transocean flying.

Arrived at New York City at twelve noon. Was delayed considerably clearing customs.

I called Flora and took a much appreciated bath. It was a great thrill to talk to my devoted wife and to tell her I would likely see her in the early morning.

We then went to the airport.

The ride to Chicago was very rough but otherwise uneventful. Left Chicago at 9:30 P.M. for Salt Lake. (ETB Journal.)

My wonderful husband called me from New York today. He just had arrived in the good old USA from Europe. He will fly from New York to Salt Lake City and be home with us again December 13 at 4:30 A.M.

I can hardly wait for my adorable husband to arrive. I don't believe I can sleep at all tonight. It is seven o'clock in the evening now, and if the airplane is on time, he will be here in nine-and-one-half more hours. (FAB Journal.)

PART 3:
HOME AGAIN

Friday, the thirteenth, has been anything but unlucky! (ETB Journal.)

FRIDAY, DECEMBER 13, 1946
SALT LAKE CITY, UTAH

We arrived in Salt Lake at 6:00 A.M. There, to my joy and our mutual satisfaction, I was greeted by my sweet and ever-loving and faithful wife on the very spot where we stood and said farewell exactly ten-and-a-half months ago.

She was so lovely in her red coat and black hat, and it was a soul-satisfying experience to take her in my arms again in affectionate embrace.

We rode home slowly in our lovely new Pontiac Six to greet the four lovely daughters, all in nightgowns as they had just arisen from their beds.

Then began a day of sweet reunions and loving association. In the late afternoon Reed and Mark came in from Provo, and we had a delightful evening, interrupted only by newspaper interviews and photographs at the home.

But even on retirement, Flora and I talked, planned, and dreamed until near daybreak. It is such a joy to be

232

home and we all thank the Lord for his watchcare and the lovely reunion we all prize so much. (ETB Journal.)

SATURDAY, DECEMBER 14, 1946:
SALT LAKE CITY, UTAH

This morning with Flora I had brief conferences with President J. Reuben Clark and President George Albert Smith separately in the way of preliminary report. They advised me to take several days away from the office, to take some much needed rest, and to see Flora safely through her operation.

The Lord, through his priesthood, has pronounced rich blessings upon her head, and while I could wish it were not necessary, I know the Lord will direct all things for our best good and will see her safely through this ordeal.

Flora is so fearless and full of love and faith. I hope and pray all will be well and she will be fully restored to health. We all love and need her so very much.

Spent the afternoon with the family and at my desk at home. (ETB Journal.)

SUNDAY, DECEMBER 15, 1946:
SALT LAKE CITY, UTAH

This has been a joyous day of reunion with my family. Flora and I conducted a Sunday School in our home for our children and their friends because of no Sunday School in the ward due to a breakdown in the heating plant. (ETB Journal.)

THURSDAY, DECEMBER 19, 1946:
SALT LAKE CITY, UTAH

The past four days have been filled with conferences, greetings, and personal matters. It has been a real joy to renew acquaintance with my associates of the General Authorities, many of whom I saw for the first time since my return at the lovely Beneficial Life Insurance party.

Today I was privileged to meet with the counselors in

the Presidency and the Twelve, except Stephen L Richards, who is sick, in our weekly temple meeting. It is a real joy to be again in the temple of the Lord. The prayers of the Brethren on behalf of my devoted wife, who faces a serious operation, brought tears of gratitude. (ETB Journal.)

WEDNESDAY, DECEMBER 25, 1946:
SALT LAKE CITY, UTAH

This has been a glorious day from the very moment little Flora Beth led the children into our lovely living room to find what Santa had left on and under each chair. (We have followed the same custom I knew as a boy of having a chair for each child lined up in a row with a stocking hanging on each one and the larger presents placed on, under, and in front.) The children were most happy and appreciative. There has not been an unkind word all day. In fact, we seldom hear them in our home. But this day has been especially blessed, for which I am most grateful. It has been such a joy to sit with my angel wife and review the past, devoid of regrets, anticipate the future joyously, and count our many blessings gratefully.

I shall never forget this glorious Christmas. It may be several years before we're all together at Christmastime. We are planning missions for the boys—followed by more college, possibly in the east, so it was a day to bring forth gratitude.

I know of no finer family, as measured by LDS standards, in all the world. There are larger and no doubt more brilliant families but, I am sure, no children of which parents could be more proud and grateful. (ETB Journal.)

SUNDAY, DECEMBER 29, 1946:
SALT LAKE CITY, UTAH

The past five days have largely been spent with the family and taking care of private affairs and making plans for my wife to go to the hospital. A goodly part of the time has been spent at the telephone receiving welcome-home greetings from friends and loved ones and giving counsel to welfare workers and Saints with relatives in Europe.

Drove Flora to the hospital in preparation for the major operation she is to undergo tomorrow. Mark E. Petersen joined me and we administered to Flora. There was a sweet, heavenly spirit present, and the same priceless promises were sealed upon her head as were pronounced by Brother Harold B. Lee in November when he administered to her at my request from London by telephone. We feel reassured all will be well with her. (ETB Journal.)

MONDAY, DECEMBER 30, 1946:
SALT LAKE CITY, UTAH

My darling wife was three hours in the operating room today. I was with her and witnessed part of the operation from the balcony but later left when informed I was breaking hospital rules.

Never have I seen any person face a major operation with such faith, cheerful confidence, and assurance. She waved good-bye and smiled sweetly as she was wheeled into the room.

She struggled considerably as she came out of the anesthetic and later was in intense pain, eased only by hypos. In the evening she was more like herself but was still suffering distress. (ETB Journal.)

TUESDAY, DECEMBER 31, 1946:
SALT LAKE CITY, UTAH

Time today divided about equally at home, the office, and the hospital. Flora seems much improved as I make this entry at 10:15 P.M., although she has suffered much distress most of the day.

Everyone is most kind bringing food to the home, flowers to the hospital, and offering to help in any way possible. So many kind inquiries by telephone and in person have come for which we are grateful.

As I close this volume, I sit in my lovely home in the

quiet of a peaceful winter's night. It is a bit lonely with Flora, my ever-faithful wife whom I love most dearly, at the hospital.

I am deeply grateful for all the Lord's rich blessings and especially for the gospel, the blessings of the holy apostleship, the glorious blessings received through the priesthood in the house of the Lord, and for my faithful wife and six choice children. For the material blessings and comforts I am also most thankful.

This has no doubt been the most eventful year of my life to date. I have traveled well over 65,000 miles, often at great natural hazards, through war-torn countries—in the air most of the way, including two air trips across the Atlantic and in most all of the nations of Europe. In it all I've been protected and richly sustained. I am grateful for it all and for the rich blessings which have attended my family during my absence.

Although I have been put to many inconveniences and hardships, so called, because of the devastation of war, yet I feel sure my ever-faithful and devoted wife has had the hardest end of the mission. She has been true blue in every respect, and I'm grateful for her, the unity in my family, and their constant support without the least murmur.

The Lord be praised for all his mercy and goodness. I hope and pray constantly I can so serve him so as to prove, in part at least, worthy of these rich blessings. (ETB Journal.)

APPENDIX A:
SETTING APART BLESSING

Brother Ezra Taft Benson, in the authority of the holy priesthood, we lay our hands upon your head and we set you apart to preside over the European Mission of The Church of Jesus Christ of Latter-day Saints.

We bless you with every power and gift necessary to enable you to go to your field of labor and accomplish the work—putting the missions of Europe in order and accomplishing that which is so important to be done at this time.

Inasmuch as it was deemed advisable for you to go by air, we bless you that you may feel comfortable, that you may go safely, that you may arrive at your destination and assume the full responsibility that will be yours.

There is a great transformation going on in these nations to which you go. There are many people who will need encouragement. It will be your responsibility to counsel frequently with the men who are called upon to preside in the various nations and to keep close to the field until every organization is in satisfactory condition and you will be able to report all is well.

There are millions of our Father's children in those lands who need to know of the gospel of Jesus Christ. There are many of them who, if they understood the truth, would accept it and make preparation for eternal life in the celestial kingdom.

The responsibility on your shoulders is very great, but if you will keep close to the Lord and follow the whisperings of the still, small voice that will be with you constantly, you will see a development over there—an increase in membership and in happiness among the people.

We bless you that, inasmuch as you are leaving your family behind, you may have peace in your soul, realizing that they are in the keeping of the Master of heaven and earth and that they will be safeguarded as well while you are away as if you were at home.

You will find some of the membership of the Church in those lands that will be upset and disturbed and perhaps difficult to reach, but if you keep in mind they are the children of the Lord and it is your privilege to advise and counsel them, and if you will do so under the inspiration of his power, you will be surprised how many of these will be brought into full fellowship and service in that distressed part of the world.

We bless you that you may have health and strength, that you may have power of body and mind and the inspiration of the Almighty to carry on—that day by day you may feel his presence and feel that he knows where you are and what you need.

We bless you that you may have great influence with men of prominence, those who are in command in the various nations, that you may have ability to break down the prejudice that exists in many cases, that you may be warned of the attempt of the adversary to hedge up the way, and that you will be able to avoid the obstacles that are intended to prevent you from doing your work.

There is not anything desirable that you will not be able to do with the aid and the help of the Lord, and every gift and power will be with you to accomplish his work if you will do your full part.

We bless you now that you may have peace in your soul, that you may feel from day to day that sacred nearness to our Heavenly Father that will make you happy and give you joy.

Keep your secretary close to you in your travels. We bless you that you may be able to retain the influences that direct you both that happiness will be with you.

Do not jeopardize your life. Do not expose yourself unnecessarily to the assaults of the adversary, because he will be anxious to prevent you from doing the work that you are going to do. But remember that if it is necessary to appeal to the Lord and the circumstances justify, you can go to him with full confidence because you will be acting under his direction and under the inspiration of his Spirit and will be given strength to accomplish everything that is necessary to be done.

A great development is about to occur in that land, and the gospel will be preached in parts of it where we have not been able to go until now. It will be your responsibility to be alert and take advantage of every opportunity.

Keep us posted here at headquarters that we may counsel and advise with you, that everything that is done may be done in a pleasing way to our Heavenly Father.

Every blessing that you desire will be yours to enable you to accomplish your responsibility.

We renew upon you the promises that have been made heretofore not yet fulfilled and say to you: Go in peace. Rejoice in this great blessing that has come to you to represent our Heavenly Father in that land. Be happy and contented and satisfied in shaping the destiny of the missionary work over there as the days go by.

We say unto you: Peace, happiness, assurance, strength in every way be upon you.

We bless you to the end that you may accomplish this most important work and in the due time of our Heavenly Father return to your loved ones in peace and safety with the favor of the Lord resting upon you.

To this end we devote you to this service of the Master and set you apart for this mission and bless you that it may be a happy experience, in the name of Jesus Christ. Amen.

APPENDIX B:
FAREWELL – GOD BLESS YOU!

FAREWELL MESSAGE OF PRESIDENT EZRA TAFT BENSON
TO THE SAINTS AND FRIENDS OF THE EUROPEAN MISSION

To the Saints, my beloved brethren and sisters, friends, and people generally throughout the European Mission: Greetings.

Regretfully, but with a heart overflowing with gratitude, I take leave of the elders, Saints, and the populace and retire from the presidency of the European Mission.

On February 4, 1946 – twenty-one days after the announcement of my appointment to this honorable position by the First Presidency of the Church – I landed in England by airplane, accompanied by my secretary and faithful companion, Elder Frederick W. Babbel.

My regrets are all for the parting now in prospect – a parting with the kind, loving friends I have made in and out of the Church during my sojourn of more than ten months among you.

My gratitude springs from an unshakable knowledge that the Almighty has opened the way and prepared the path before me and that mission presidents, elders, Saints, and friends have extended their loving help and cooperation throughout the difficult months following the world's greatest war of destruction – centering, as it has, within the boundaries of the European Mission.

Elder Alma Sonne, Assistant to the Council of the Twelve – a true and faithful servant of the Lord and a lover of humanity – has been appointed by the First Presidency to preside in Europe.

He has already arrived, and together we have made brief visits to ten of the twelve missions which comprise the European Mission. I bespeak for him the same loyal support, love, and esteem that have always been shown toward me. All future communications pertaining to the missions should be directed to President Sonne.

In the providence of the Lord, I am now to return to my mountain home where my ever-faithful wife, children, and other loved ones await me, and I shall be privileged again to enjoy the priceless association of the Brethren in the presiding councils of the Church.

As I bid you adieu, there passes before me a panoramic view of the unprecedented experiences of the past few months. These have been both heartrending and soul-satisfying. They have made impressions that will remain so long as time shall last. It has been a sobering, thought-provoking period.

With the terrible ravages of war on every side — the result of man's sinful disobedience of the commandments of the Lord — and man's wicked misuse of the bounties of nature — one is made to exclaim: "O, God, how long will thy children continue their inhuman slaughter of their fellowmen? How long will the leaders of nations pursue the futile destruction of war? When will the suffering of little children, old men and women, and innocent people everywhere cease and they be called upon no longer to endure the ravages of fiends in human form? When will men and nations learn the way of peace and the futility of bloody conflict?"

Amidst all the terrible aftermath of war, the contact with the Saints in all the war-torn countries has been a sad, though inspiring, experience. Here we have witnessed the fruits of the restored gospel in the lives of our members. We have not been disappointed.

Here we have found faith, loyalty, and devotion unsurpassed in the annals of Church history. Only through a testimony that God lives and has revealed himself from heaven and established his Church can men and women stand amidst the rubble which was once happy homes with hope and courage.

Only with a faith in the ultimate consummation of the Lord's purposes can people, with all their earthly possessions swept away, continue with spirits sweet and hearts free from bitterness.

241

No man-made organization or set of dogmas can make people look hopefully forward with confident faith as they stand—the only remaining member of a once happy and prosperous family.

Thank God for the testimony which our Saints possess! It has been theirs all during the dark days of war. This alone, with the sweet companionship of the Holy Spirit, has sustained them. Nothing else is so precious. With this faith and testimony, they have carried on with their meetings in bombed-out churches, homes, and in the open air. With this faith they have been united—they have sustained each other. They have, in very deed, been their brother's keeper.

And so to the Saints throughout Europe I say: God bless you. I love you beyond my power of expression. I have been happiest when mingling with you in sweet communion, blessed with the presence of the Spirit of the Lord.

As I have traveled among you—traveling over 50,000 miles during the past ten months—I have been grateful to shake your hands, to look into your eyes, and to know you are in very deed my brethren and sisters in the true fold of the Church of Jesus Christ.

I shall never forget your love and the many acts of kindness, extending even to personal acts of affection for my loyal wife and companion, whom you have never seen. Your evidences of faith and love are more precious than riches. These acts are engraven upon my heart forever. Gratefully do I acknowledge your loving kindness to me as a servant of Jesus Christ. Our Father in Heaven will also have your acts in remembrance.

I bless you in the name of the Lord and promise you the richest blessings of eternity inasmuch as you continue faithful. Be not cast down, dear brethren and sisters. Let not your faith waver. God still rules. He is at the helm. He has not forgotten you, nor will he do so if you keep sacred your covenants as members of his Church. Therefore, as he has said to his Saints, "Fear not, little flock; do good; let earth and hell combine against you, for if ye are built upon my rock, they cannot prevail." So let it be.

And if the clouds gather for a moment, be assured that behind every cloud for you there is a smiling Providence.

"What tho the clouds seem dark today,
Tomorrow's will be blue.

When every cloud has cleared away.
God's providence shines through."

Be true to every standard and teaching of the Church. Support loyally your mission, district, and branch presidents and other officers. Cease from all evil speaking and faultfinding. Be united. Keep the Sabbath day holy. Pay your tithes and offerings. Attend to your family and secret prayers daily. Give freely of your time, means, and talents for the building up of the kingdom of God in the earth. Be kind to your families. Be pure in mind and body. Keep the Spirit of God in your homes and in your hearts. Be wise and prudent as you go forward with energy and determination to fill the full measure of your creation in the earth. Perform with soberness, but with happy and joyous hearts, the work at hand, knowing that all is well if we live righteously.

Do all this, and eventually you shall be exalted on high and triumph over all your enemies. There, I trust, in that eternal world we shall meet in sweet reunion where war and sin are no more, in the sweet fellowship which we have but tasted here. If we are worthy, it shall be so, which I fervently pray for us all.

And now before leaving this hemisphere to return home, I feel to direct a few words of solemn warning to the nations, rulers, and peoples of the countries through which I have traveled. Having been called and sent of God, this is done in the spirit of humility and with a recognition that we are all children of our Heavenly Father and that He desires to bless us. But he cannot look upon sin with the least degree of allowance. Great calamities for the nations are impending. There is only one way of escape. It is the way the God of this earth has provided.

To the rulers and peoples of these European nations, I solemnly declare that the God of heaven has established his latter-day kingdom upon the earth in fulfillment of prophecies uttered by his ancient prophets and apostles. Holy angels have again communed with men on the earth. God has again revealed himself from heaven and restored to the earth his holy priesthood with power to administer in all the sacred ordinances necessary for the exaltation of his children. His Church has been reestablished among men with all the spiritual gifts enjoyed anciently.

All this is done in preparation for Christ's second coming.

The great and dreadful day of the Lord is near at hand. In preparation for this great event and as a means of escaping the impending judgments, inspired messengers have gone forth to the nations of the earth carrying this testimony and warning.

The nations of the earth continue in their sinful and un-righteous ways. The unbounded knowledge with which men have been blessed has been used to destroy mankind instead of to bless the children of men as the Lord intended. Two great world wars in the past twenty-five years, with fruitless efforts at lasting peace, are solemn evidence that peace has been taken from the earth because of the wickedness of the people. Nations cannot endure in sin. They will be broken up, but the kingdom of God will endure forever.

Therefore, as a humble servant of the Lord, I call upon the leaders of nations to humble themselves before God, to seek his inspiration and guidance. I call upon rulers and people alike to repent of their evil ways. Turn unto the Lord, seek his forgive-ness and unite yourselves in humility with his kingdom. There is no other way.

If you will do this, your sins will be blotted out, peace will come and remain, and you will become a part of the kingdom of God in preparation for Christ's second coming, which is near at hand. But if you refuse to repent or to accept the testimony of his inspired messengers and unite yourselves with God's kingdom, then the terrible judgments and calamities promised the wicked will be yours.

The Lord in his mercy has provided a way of escape. The voice of warning is to all people by the mouths of his servants. If this voice is not heeded, the angels of destruction will go forth again and the chastening hand of Almighty God will be felt upon the nations, as decreed, until a full end thereof will be the result. Wars, devastation, and untold suffering will be your lot except you turn unto the Lord in humble repentance. Destruction, even more terrible and far-reaching than attended the war just ended, will come with certainty unless rulers and people alike repent and cease their evil and godless ways.

God will not be mocked. He will not permit sins of immo-rality, thievery, deceit, Sabbath-breaking, and disregard for all his holy commandments and the messages of his servants to go unheeded without grievous punishment for such wickedness.

The nations of Europe and of the world cannot endure in sin. The way of escape is clear. The immutable laws of God remain steadfastly in the heavens above. When men and nations refuse to abide by them, the penalty must follow. They will be wasted away. Sin cannot endure.

And now, although I have been permitted to bear my humble testimony verbally in thirteen of the European nations before thousands of people, I desire to bear it once more through the medium of the various mission organs. I know that God lives, the he is a personal Being, the Father of our spirits, and that he loves his children and hears and answers their righteous prayers.

I know that it is his will that his children be happy. It is his desire to bless us all. I know that Jesus Christ is the Son of God, our elder brother, the very Creator and Redeemer of the world. I know that God has again established his kingdom on the earth in fulfillment of prophecy and that it will never be overcome, but it shall ultimately hold universal dominion in the earth and Jesus Christ shall reign as its king forever.

I know that God in his goodness has again revealed himself from the heavens and that Joseph Smith was called of God to reestablish that kingdom. I testify that he accomplished this work, that he laid the foundations, and that he committed to the Church the keys and powers to continue the great latter-day work, which he began under the direction of Almighty God.

I know that Joseph Smith, although slain as a martyr to the truth, still lives and that as head of this dispensation — the greatest of all dispensations — he will continue so to stand throughout the eternities to come. He is a prophet of God, a seer, and a revelator, as are his successors.

I know that the inspiration of the Lord is directing the Church today because I have felt of its power. I know that the First Presidency and other General Authorities of the Church have as their object and purpose the glory of God and the exaltation of his children.

And finally, I know that no person who does not receive this work can be saved in the celestial kingdom of God and escape the condemnation of the Judge of us all.

Humbly and prayerfully I leave this testimony, knowing full well I must eventually meet my Maker and stand with all men before the judgment bar of God. More than anything else in all

245

the world, I am grateful for this testimony of the divinity of this great latter-day work and exhort all men everywhere to give heed thereto.

And now a fond farewell and God bless you!

APPENDIX C:
REPORT OF MISSION
TO GENERAL CONFERENCE

GENERAL CONFERENCE ADDRESS
OF ELDER EZRA TAFT BENSON
SUNDAY, APRIL 6, 1947

Through seven inspirational sessions I have not lost faith that my time would come.

To one who has spent the major part of the last year amidst the rubble and destruction of war-torn Europe, this conference has been doubly inspirational and appreciated. As I have looked into the faces of this well-fed (almost too well-fed, in many cases) audience, well-clothed, surrounded with all the comforts and blessings of life, I have found that my thoughts have many times drifted across the Atlantic to those of our brethren and sisters with whom I have been closely associated during recent months. I love them, my brethren and sisters, as I am sure you do, many of you having descended through progenitors from those nations.

We have heard much in this conference regarding Europe and the Latter-day Saints in those countries. You heard testimonies from two of the former mission presidents of those missions who told of the suffering of the Saints and who bore fervent testimony to the faithfulness and devotion of Latter-day Saints in Europe. You heard from Brother Frederick W. Babbel, my companion and faithful associate, regarding his observations in Europe. If the Lord will bless me during the next few moments,

247

I should like, in keeping with the suggestion of President Smith, to refer briefly to some of the phases in connection with observations and travels in Europe, covering a period of some ten months and more than sixty thousand miles.

I hasten to suggest, my brethren and sisters, that even though many fine comments were made regarding our mission over there, I assure you I know the source of the success which attended our labors. Never at any time have I felt it would be possible for me or my associates to accomplish the mission to which we were assigned without the directing power of the Almighty.

I shall never forget my feelings when I read in the press the announcement by the First Presidency regarding our call. The magnitude of it seemed ovewhelming. They gave us a four-point charge: first, to attend to the spiritual affairs of the Church in Europe; second, to work to make available food, clothing, and bedding to our suffering Saints in all parts of Europe; third, to direct the reorganization of the various missions of Europe; and, fourth, to prepare for the return of missionaries to those countries.

Our great desire was to live so that the Lord would bless us in carrying out those directions, and I testify to you this afternoon, my brethren and sisters, that the Lord has in very deed blessed us on every turn. He has gone before us. Barriers have melted away. Problems that seemed impossible to solve have been solved, and the work in large measure has been accomplished through the blessings of the Lord.

I remember well our first inquiry as to the time we could set sail, either by plane or boat. We were told it would take three months—that all bookings were filled for that period. Yet within twenty-one days from the time our appointment was announced, we landed at Hurn Airport sixty miles south of London. And in spite of a most acute housing shortage in London, two days thereafter suitable headquarters had been established; how, I do not know, except through the blessings of the Almighty; and had we been free to select a spot for our headquarters, as it developed later, we could not have done better for our purpose. And so today I am grateful beyond my power of expression for the blessings that have accompanied us on our mission in Europe.

I am grateful for the love of the Saints over there, and for their devotion, for their faith, for the manner in which they received us. They are a great people. I have never seen greater faith anywhere in the Church than we saw among the Saints in the war-torn countries.

I will not take time today to describe the terrors of war, the worst of which is not the physical combat but that which follows—the abandonment of moral and religious restraints; the increase in sin, disease; the increase in infant mortality; and all the suffering which accompanies famine, disease, and immorality. We saw these things on every side. We saw nations prostrate, flat on their backs economically. We found it difficult even to get a telephone call through from London to many of our missions on the continent when we arrived. We could not even make a telephone call to Holland, let alone countries like Poland, Czechoslovakia, and other nations. Almost the only type of transportation available was that under the control of the military. But through the blessings of the Lord we were able within eight days to make our first trip to the continent, and from Paris made our journey into the various nations of Europe.

I think I shall never forget those first meetings with the Saints. They have suffered much, my brethren and sisters. We wondered just how they would receive us, what the reaction would be. Would their hearts be filled with bitterness? Would there be hatred there? Would they have soured on the Church? I well remember our first meeting at Karlsruhe. After we had made visits through Belgium, Holland, and the Scandinavian countries, we went into occupied Germany. We finally found our way to the meeting place, a partially bombed-out building located in the interior of a block. The Saints had been in session for some two hours waiting for us, hoping that we would come because the word had reached them that we might be there for the conference. And then for the first time in my life I saw almost an entire audience in tears as we walked up onto the platform, and they realized that at last, after six or seven long years, representatives from Zion, as they put it, had finally come back to them. Then as the meeting closed, prolonged at their request, they insisted we go to the door and shake hands with each one of them as they left the bombed-out building. And we noted that many of them, after they had passed through the line, went

249

back and came through the second and third time, so happy were they to grasp our hands. As I looked into their upturned faces, pale, thin, many of these Saints dressed in rags, some of them barefooted, I could see the light of faith in their eyes as they bore testimony to the divinity of this great latter-day work, and expressed their gratitude for the blessings of the Lord.

That is what a testimony does. We saw it in many countries. I say there is no greater faith, to my knowledge, anywhere in the Church than we found among those good people in Europe.

Many interesting things happened as you can well imagine. Ofttimes our meeting rooms were in almost total darkness as we were forced to close the windows, filled with cardboard instead of glass, because of a rainstorm. But the Saints insisted that we go on with the meeting. Other times we would close a meeting, and then they would ask if we could not hold another before we sent them home—they were so happy to have the opportunity of meeting with us. I remember in Nuremberg that the people had waited two hours for us—we were delayed because of detours around bombed bridges and other things. Shortly after we arrived, the curfew rang, but they requested that we allow them to stay on; and after the meeting was over, they were forced to stay all night in the old partially bombed-out schoolhouse because of curfew restrictions. Words cannot adequately express the joy of the Saints for the first missionwide conference following the war in England, Holland, Sweden, and other countries.

We found that our members had carried on in a marvelous way. Their faith was strong, their devotion greater, and their loyalty unsurpassed. We found very little, if any, bitterness or despair.

There was a spirit of fellowship and brotherhood which had extended from one mission to the other, and as we traveled, the Saints asked us to take their greetings to their brothers and sisters in other countries although their nations had been at war only a few months before. Local missionaries had carried on during the war period. In some districts there had been more baptisms than during a comparable period prior to the war.

They had lived the standards of the Church. The Word of Wisdom has been a great blessing to them. Whereas many people, driven by the pangs of hunger, had had their desire for

250

tobacco intensified and would trade their meager food allowance for more tobacco, the Saints traded their rations of tobacco for more food. Truly this revelation of over one hundred years ago is a great blessing to them.

They have suffered much, my brethren and sisters. You heard President Clark read a letter here on Friday from President Walter Stover in Berlin. You may think that is an isolated case. It is only one of hundreds, many of which are much worse than the one he referred to, because our Saints in some cases have suffered more than death. It is worse than death for a mother or a father to have to stand at the point of a gun while they witness their little thirteen- and fourteen-year-old daughters being ravished by fiends in human form. Some of our Saints were forced to go through that.

Yes, they have been hungry; they have been cold. We saw many such families long before welfare supplies arrived in Europe. Thank God that the welfare supplies are there now!

Our local mission presidents have performed a marvelous work. The local leaders, district and branch presidents, have done yeoman service for which we are deeply grateful to them. The local people have rallied around and supported them in every way.

Probably the saddest part of our mission was with our refugees. These poor, unwanted souls have been driven from their once happy homes to destinations unknown. They came with all their earthly possessions on their backs, but after organizing them into branches, calling them into meetings, they sang the songs of Zion with a fervor I am sure has never been surpassed. We visited some of their homes — their shacks — where as many as twenty-two people were living in one room — four complete families! And yet they knelt together in prayer night and morning and bore testimony to us regarding the blessings of the gospel.

Now just a word about the welfare program. I bring to you, my brethren and sisters, the deep gratitude and thanksgiving of the Saints in Europe. The spirit of the welfare program was there long before we arrived. The Saints in various countries had sent help to their less fortunate brothers and sisters in other nations. Welfare gardens had been planted. We found them among the bombed-out buildings. We ran on to many instances where following bombings, branches had joined together and

251

pooled all their remaining supplies, food, clothing, and household articles, and turned them over to the priesthood for distribution according to need.

It was a great joy when the welfare supplies came through. It was also a great surprise to the military authorities and others to learn with what dispatch the supplies arrived from Zion, after arrangements were made, and the cable sent back to Zion, March 24, 1946, to start shipments. They could hardly believe that there was a Church in existence with a hundred storehouses well stocked, ready to dispatch supplies to the suffering people in Europe. You have heard figures regarding the quantities that have arrived—some fifty-one carloads. That means over two hundred European carloads, or approximately two thousand tons, and I am sure that if the cost of transporting it on the European end was considered, it would total well over three quarters of a million dollars. The bulk of that, of course, has gone to the countries in greatest distress—Germany, Austria, Holland, Norway, Belgium—with quantities going to many other countries according to need.

I have faced congregations of more than a thousand Latter-day Saints where it was estimated by the mission president that more than 80 percent of the total clothing worn was clothing from Zion, sent through the welfare program. My brethren and sisters, do you need any further evidence of the need for this program and the inspiration back of it? I wish you could have spent a few days with me in Europe during this past year. I tell you God is directing this program. It is inspired! Had it not been so, there would have been many, many hundreds more of our Latter-day Saints perish with hunger and die of cold because of the lack of simple food commodities and clothing.

Now the work is going forward in Europe. New buildings are being provided. Under the direction of the First Presidency, purchases have been made in Sweden, England, and Holland of buildings and lots. New headquarters have been established and the work of the Lord is progressing. We have fine cooperation from the military authorities, from civic, business, and professional people. Our United States embassies have cooperated fully. The radio and the press have been friendly. And on the whole, with mission presidents now back in all of the missions, except the West German Mission and permission granted for a president to go there, with four hundred and fifty missionaries already called and assigned and one hundred others waiting for visas, the outlook is encouraging. Even in Germany and Austria, where missionaries have not been permitted to go in numbers, some seventy local missionaries are serving full time to carry on the great work.

Two distributions of welfare supplies have been made in all districts in Germany and in the East German Mission; a third distribution was made through purchases on the Swiss market before welfare supplies arrived. A third distribution is now being made in the western zones which comprise the West German Mission. In Holland and Norway the work is progressing equally well.

While the outlook for the Church is favorable in Europe if peace can be maintained, certainly the outlook for the world at large is anything but encouraging. After two years, following the second world war in twenty-five years, the world is indeed in a sorry state. Once powerful nations in Europe, Asia, and the Orient are flat on their backs—industries broken, economies shattered, and their once-happy people on starvation doles. A large part of the world is cold, hungry, and desperate. Millions without the gospel are without hope. Europe today is in the midst of one of the greatest ideological conflicts in recorded human history—whether government exists for the individual or the individual for the government. We feel it only vaguely here, but it is real. To me the threat of godless communism is a stern reality, not only in Europe but also in blessed America.

The outlook for the world is not encouraging, but we know what the answer is. There is only one answer, and that is the gospel of Jesus Christ. Peace must come from the heart. Men's hearts must change, and righteousness must rule in the lives of the people of the world before peace can come. May God hasten the day. May the message of the restored gospel go forward in great force, by increasing numbers, that God's children may escape the calamities which are impending, I humbly pray in the name of Jesus Christ. Amen.

INDEX

supports husband in mission call, 7-8; receives blessing from husband, 10; devotion and faith of, 11; describes husband's departure, 13-14; photographs of, 14, 82; expresses appreciation for husband, 18, 169; independent nature of, 21, 60; sends pie recipe to husband, 43; sends boxes of food, 53, 88, 110, 139; cares for sick baby, 58-59, 76-77; sends gum and candy for children, 59-60; receives telephone calls from husband, 74-76, 108-9, 175, 185, 193, 207, 231; attends general conference, 79, 81, 198; entertains Danish couple, 82-83; celebrates Mother's Day, 98-99; postpones operation, 109, 201-2, 209-10, 211; attends John H. Taylor's funeral, 113; attends June conference, 116; attends General Authorities' party, 134-35; celebrates birthday, 137-38; participates in temple sealings, 180; wedding anniversary of, 185-86; feelings of, about children, 202; expresses gratitude for blessings, 203-4, 213; needs operation promptly, 206-7; receives blessing from Elder Lee, 209; bears testimony about supporting husband, 220-21; President Benson praises support of, 228-29; anticipates husband's arrival, 230, 231; reunion of, with husband, 232-33; undergoes operation, 235

Benson, Flora Beth. *See* Benson, Beth

Benson, Mark, 10, 12, 82, 87, 96, 115, 232

Benson, Reed, 10, 12-13, 82, 87, 115, 134, 232

Bergen, Norway, 93

Berlin, Germany: refugees fleeing to, 41-42; President Benson travels to, 56-57, 125, 152; devastation of, 57-58, 60, 64-66; viewing Hitler's headquarters in, 64, 69; President Benson meets with Saints in, 65, 126, 153-54; emergency supplies for, 127; arrival of welfare products in, 191, 205; taking leave of Saints in, 223

Berndt, Otto, 121

Bielefeld, Germany, 42

Bing, Captain, 114

Birmingham, England, 198-99

Black market, 50-51, 65, 123, 167, 187; controlling, through new currency, 189

Blessings: President Benson gives, to family, 10; setting apart President Benson, 11, 237-39; given to sick Benson baby, 53, 58; given to Sister Benson, 209

Blomquist, Eben R. T., 98, 102, 145, 149, 180, 182, 218-19

Book of Mormon: need for copies of, 128; copies of, arrive in Berlin, 191

Boy Scouts, 116-17

Boyer, Selvoy J., 85, 107, 138; Sister Benson speaks with, 90, 93, 95; is injured in accident, 186; improving condition of, 194; meets with Presidents Benson and Sonne, 216

Bremen, Germany, 55, 118-19

Breslau, Poland, 156-58

Brinton, Captain, 38

presidents at, 54; meetings of Saints in, 55, 124-25

Heidelberg, Germany, 46-47

Helsinki, Finland, 146

Herne, Germany, 129

Hitler, headquarters of, 64, 69

Holland: relief packages sent to, 8; President Benson travels to, 24-25, 80; condition of Church in, 25-26

Hoover, Herbert, 84

House of Commons, 114

Howells, Adele C., 84

International Conference of Agriculture Producers, 106-7, 108, 109, 111-13

International Red Cross, 45, 46, 118-19, 127, 136, 176

Ivalo, M. Asko, 147

Jakobstad, Finland, 143-44, 145

Jeske, Max, 223

Jews: slaughter of, 168; return of, to Palestine, 182-83

Johansen, Alf, 184

Johansson, C. Fritz, 30-31, 101

Karlsruhe, Germany, 41-43

Kiel, Germany, 117-18, 123

Kimball, Camilla, 14, 23

Kimball, Spencer W., 13, 14, 53

Kleinert, Jean, 22

"K-Ration Quartet," 74, 75

Kristianborg Castle, 181-82

Kvinnesdal, Norway, 94

Lane, Bliss, Ambassador, 169

Langen, Germany, 130-32, 222

Langheinrich, Paul, 61-62, 64, 223

Larsmo, Finland, 144-45

Lee, Fern, 14, 66

Lee, Harold B., 7, 12, 66, 84; blesses Benson baby, 58; gives

blessing to Sister Benson, 209, 211

Leipzig, Germany, 125-26

Lemon pie recipe, 43

Libera, Kazenurg, Dr., 223

Liege, Belgium, 78

Liverpool, England, 201

London: President Benson sets up operations in, 19-20; office in, President Benson works in, 35, 85-86, 138-39, 178; Gold and Green Ball in, 115-16

Madame Tussaud's wax works, 203

Marriages: performed in blacksmith shop, 90; incorrect procedures in, 99

McKay, Emma Ray, 70

McKay, Thomas E., 2-3, 7, 81

McNarney, Joseph T., General, 35, 47-49, 222

Meik, Vivian, 202-3

Merrill, Eugene, 152, 169, 171, 222

Merrill, Joseph F., 152

Mikolajozuk, Stanislaw, 160

Missionaries: urgent need for, 105; seeking admission of, into Europe, 172; President Benson meets with, 199-200; arrival of, in the Netherlands, 217

Missionary work: vigorous program of, in Germany, 62; in Czechoslovakia, 69, 70, 137; prospects for, hampered by food situation, 97; prospects for, in Scandinavia, 101-2, 103, 106; monument commemorating beginning of, 137; dedicating Finland for, 144-45; prospects for, in Finland, 147, 149; potential for, in Poland, 170, 173

261